Praise for *My Animal Life*

'A living and unusual book: part social history, part family history and part autobiography which chronicles the evolution and career of a gifted novelist. Observant, honest and sensitively written ... it demands to be read.'

Michael Holroyd

'Exceptionally interesting and brave ... Maggie Gee's account of her life as a writer cuts to the bone as she relives triumphs, rejections, despair and renewal. It's a wonderful book, for its boldness and vigour, and for its piercing honesty.'

Claire Tomalin

'*My Animal Life* is full of riches. [Maggie Gee] writes with uncompromising honesty about the triumphs and vicissitudes of her personal and literary life and offers balanced and wise insights into family and friendship, motherhood and marriage, class and race. Highly recommended for all aspiring writers.'

Bernardine Evaristo

'Maggie Gee writes with such courage and wit. This is a vivid portrait of a woman finding her way through the maze of class-ridden, post-war England, the 60s, feminism and how to be a mother and a writer.'

Diana Melly

Books by Maggie Gee

Novels
Dying in Other Words
The Burning Book
Light Years
Grace
Where are the Snows
Lost Children
The Ice People
The White Family
The Flood
My Cleaner
My Driver

Short Stories
The Blue

Maggie Gee

My Animal Life

TELEGRAM

This edition published in 2010 by Telegram

ISBN: 978-1-84659-987-3

A full CIP record for this book is available from the British Library.
A full CIP record for this book is available from the Library of Congress.

Printed and bound by Thomson Press Ltd (India)

TELEGRAM
26 Westbourne Grove, London W2 5RH, UK
2398 Doswell Avenue, Saint Paul, Minnesota, 55108, US
Verdun, Beirut, Lebanon
www.telegrambooks.com

To my family

1 My animal luck (i)

here today
gone tomorrow

I am alive at the time of writing this. And so are you. For nearly four billion years of life on earth, neither of us existed: we were a blank. For the next few billion years before the sun burns up the earth, our bodies will be bones under the ground, or ash, asleep.

But now, in this astonishing living moment, we are between two states of non-being, two endless nights. Unprepared, we are thrust on stage. The light is on, the eye open. Life! Brains and muscles, feathers and fur! From nothing, we are ourselves, moving and breathing, here. Suddenly, this is our chance; our luck, our animal luck.

(After my mother died, one of the sayings she liked, 'This is not a dress rehearsal', ran through and through my head. It would come to me at opportune moments: when about to have a tiff with my husband at a motorway service station, say. *Mustn't waste time being unhappy.*)

As I sit in the window writing this, house-martins swoop like acrobats, sunlit then shadowed, up under the eaves above my head, dip and swoop, dip and swoop, white bellies, black wings that flare into brief transparency with the blaze of the sun behind them, elegant licks of black at quick heads and brief V-for-Victory tails. Go, martins! Enjoy your luck! They are scooping up insects in headlong flight, the day's warm on their breasts, they have young to feed.

Today in the chapel at St Cuthman's, the retreat where I have come to write, the priest said, 'God did not make you for the dark of death, but to live.'

Four days before I came here, I was in St Mary's Hospital, Paddington, having a gastroscopy for sudden unexplained stomach pains. They started at Christmas, five months ago, after a lifetime's happy eating. I had waited and worried for all that time, unable to eat as I usually do, unable to drink my evening glass of wine, losing weight, five pounds, then six, then eight, oppressed as I lay awake at night by fear, for my mother and most of her siblings died of cancer.

I found I had symptoms of everything: cholecystitis, pancreatic cancer, liver cancer, bowel cancer. There is far too much on the net about cancer. Oh virtual world of death and terror! My gloom became great: I felt relief when I found any disease that gave a chance of living five years. Five years, I computed. My daughter would be twenty-five, and might even have a child or be married; I might have written two more books. Just give me five years, and I could bear it. But quite a few of the diseases which beckoned me offered a lot less than five years. The pain was there when I ran; when I exercised at all; when I lay in bed at night. When I forgot about it, it nudged me, suddenly, a strange line of pressure right across my stomach high under my rib-cage, with a knot of discomfort on the right-hand side. And then there were the noises, great skirling borborygms that made people look at me, surprised, in meetings. (I remembered my mother: that happened to her.)

Finally, after a night when I only slept between six and seven in the morning, the date of the much-dreaded gastroscopy arrived. The greater fear, of hearing I would die, for I had read that the doctor performing the gastroscopy told you the results straight away, was diverted into smaller but equally pressing ones: that I would be unable to swallow the fibre-optic tube with the camera on the end, that I would choke – very rare, but possible, the internet hissed.

Nick came with me to the hospital. I could feel his love, for which I was grateful, and his anxiety, for which I was sorry. Though he'd been a medic on an oil rig, as a young man, he hated anything medical, anything that reminded him of what he'd rather forget, that the insides of bodies are vulnerable. But here he stood, by the St Mary's bed, smiling at me, holding my hand, asking me how to spell 'sphygmomanometer', and correcting me when I got it wrong. He had asked me, as a distraction and as part of the great game of marriage, the tiny, half-in-fun, deadly serious, up-and-down, never-ending battle for pre-eminence between two people. When we were first married – I was slightly older, and had published two books, as he had not – he discovered how sleepy and helpless I was in the morning, and would bring me breakfast, which was wonderful, and ask me questions about geography, at which I was hopeless. ('The capital of Mongolia?' 'Odessa?' 'Wrong!') Our war-games now were subtler, and the love between us twenty-five years deeper, but he could still spell sphygmomanometer, and I, at this moment, could not.

A nurse came to the bed and checked our details. 'Maggie Gee for a colonoscopy?' 'Oh no please. I'm sure it's a gastroscopy.' 'We're doing colonoscopies this morning.' 'It's a mistake,' I asserted. She looked at me, unbelieving. 'There is your name, see, on the colonoscopy list.' I looked: there it was. 'I don't care, I'm not having one.' She saw I meant business. 'I'll go and check.' Thank God, she came back and said, 'You *are* a gastroscopy but you're with the colonoscopies for some reason.'

What was the reason? I wondered in a flash of panic. Because my case was particularly bad? Would they come in through my throat, and go out through my colon, having removed all that cancerous rubbish in between? (And yet, over the two weeks before I got my appointment, the pains had definitely been lessening. Another, equally powerful jab of thought: *was it too late to leave the hospital?*)

But now a white-clad male nurse had arrived. I was spared from speculation by concrete choices. Would I have a sedative, in which case I would probably forget everything about what had happened, or not? My call. Des, the velvet-voiced, melting-eyed Irish nurse, talked as he took my blood pressure, caressing into extinction most of the syllables of the 'sphygmorrter' he was using (thus proving the point I had just made to my husband, that his precious 'sphygmomanometer' was a *bad* word that had *made* me misspell it), and seemed to hint that I should, or at any rate that he would. But half the patients did, half did not. 'I'll try without,' I decided. Be with the bolder, tougher half.

Quite soon, knees up and semi-naked on a trolley in the procedure room, I thought, 'Wrong decision', but was too embarrassed to change it. They laid me down on my left side and put a blue plastic object with a hole in it between my teeth. I remembered that I often breathed through my mouth. Today, not an option. British shyness and good manners kept me lying there, gasping, be-dummied, immobile. Then I saw it, whipping steelily about in the air like a snake to my right and above me, the infinite length of the tube I was meant to swallow, at its end the tiny camera glowing with a fierce blue light, the doctor looming behind it like a fakir, green-capped, green-gowned, faceless. I closed my eyes and gave up, remembering what had finally allowed me to fly, after years of neurotic terror, someone saying, 'You don't have to fly the plane.' Yes, I could not be in charge of this moment.

Seconds later, it was inside me. The doctor gave a would-be reassuring commentary, his tone merry and slightly manic: 'This is the worst bit, we're going over the tongue, we hmm – let's see – *YES!* and down the throat, going down now, we're in the stomach already! Now I'm going to blow some air into the stomach ... Going further down, we're in the duodenum ....'

I tried to grunt in protest, to let him know he was risking my life with this five-star itinerary, and the nurse's reassuring pressure hardened. 'You're doing very well, not long now.' 'Samples,' said the cheery maniac, 'scalpel', and then something new whizzed and pinged down the tube. 'We're just taking some biopsies, coming back now, having a good look round inside the stomach, then we'll be out.' I lay there exhausted, eyes watering, weak as a baby. 'Is it over?'

The whole thing only took five minutes. Any longer and I don't know what I would have done, but after all, what *could* I have done? By now I was no longer thinking of cancer; I was just thinking, 'Thank God he's stopped.' Small blessings, like small worries, briefly erase greater ones.

'You did well,' said the nurse. 'Don't worry. Lots of people actually fight. I had to hit one bloke quite hard.'

Not long after, the doctor, who without his mask looked young and gentle, came round the ward. I did not entirely take in what he had said, though I nodded and smiled and asked questions.

'It all looked totally normal. We didn't find anything nasty. No tumours or anything like that. The stomach looked pink and healthy. No sign of a hiatus hernia. We'll look at the samples of course.'

We didn't find anything nasty. No tumours. The stomach looked pink and healthy ...

I never got a firm diagnosis. 'Probably just an infection.' Or something to do with the extra kidney randomly discovered during those five months. How different are we all from the diagrams? What strangenesses lie under the skin?

Life. I was given it back. Not a year, not five years: no shadow. It took me several days to understand, and to shrug off the greatcoat of terror. It's a common enough experience; the mind has been told, but the body can't turn on a sixpence from one mode to another. The chemicals that are triggered by fear can't disperse on the instant. People talk about 'feeling flat' when the good news comes, of its 'not sinking in'. The body has depths; it is an ocean. How long does it take for a storm to die down?

But later, how light I felt. How light I feel. How grateful.

Outside the glass, the house-martin swoops, closer, closer, then turns on one wing and is off again, dancing away across the void. Not pinned on its back. Not ash on the ground.

When I first knew my husband, Nick was trying to get a newspaper to send him to the Falklands, where there was a war on. He had lived in Argentina, he knew Spanish. In the end, it didn't happen, and we got married. One of the great pieces of luck in my life. But he used to say then, and has often said since, always to my intense dismay, 'If I get killed in a foreign country, I want to be buried where I die.' I thought, at first, he didn't understand how sharply I would miss him and need the comfort (however bleak) of a body, or ashes, to visit.

Now I see that perhaps his wish has something to do with a life's trajectory, the distance you can travel from your starting point. Maybe an animal's life is best tracked through movement. The tiger flashing past the shadowing grasses, slipping beyond everything: sleep, death, families.

2 Why 'animal life'?

I am an animal

Why call this book *My Animal Life*?

Not to degrade my life, but to celebrate it. To join it, tiny though it is, to all the life in the universe. To the brown small-headed pheasant running by the lake in Coolham. To my grandparents and parents, and my great-grandparents who like most people in the British Isles of their generation wore big boots, even for the rare occasions of photographs, and lived on the clayey land, and have returned their bones to it, joining the bones of cattle, horses, foxes. To the blind out-of-season bee bombing the glass of this window. To link, in a way I only learned to do in my thirties, my mental life to the body I love and enjoy, to my secret sexual life and my life as a mother.

My animal life joins me, also, to my death. That mysterious thing round a bend in the road which, like every other animal stretching in the breeze and the sunlight, I wish not to know about, not yet.

I am writing this book to ask questions – to which I do not know the answer. How can we be happy? What do men want, what do women want? What do children need from us?

Can I save my belief in the soul from my love of science?

How can we bear to lose those we love most?

How do we recover from our mistakes – our many mistakes?

How do we forgive ourselves? And our parents?

Why do we need art? Why are we driven to make it?

And class: can we ever really change it?

If it seems rash to ask such questions, I have always been rash. And I am too old to be afraid.

We all ask questions something like these, silently or aloud, in pain or in hope. It is the process of asking I want to record, as the plane comes bumping down through low cloud.

Underneath, it's still there. Earth. Families. The patterns of being stamped in our nerve-ends. The long stern game of our unknown genes.

My brother John, Grandma and Grandpa Church, me

3 Two families

and which one won

Nothing about families is simple. No, wrong: there's a joy about the 'all of us are here, we are back' which begins a celebration, the joy of meeting and recognising and counting, the sense of completeness falling like balm: we're home.

How I wish they could all be here now, Mum and Dad, Gees and Churches, the uncles and aunts, shrugging off scarves and coats, fussing and laughing and settling down; in both families, hugs and kisses. The dead are with us: Uncle Arthur palms a two-bob bit and smuggles it into my pocket, Aunty Eve takes both my hands in her ring-carbuncled fingers and offers the scented dust of her cheek, little Grandma Gee comes rocking towards me like a full-bosomed sea-legged sailor, dot and carry, dot and carry, all dimples, raising her hat to release a thin froth of curled white hair, but, suddenly fretful, calls, 'Pa! Pa! will you hang this up?' – her small navy head-hugging straw hat with the long pearl hatpin – but he is too busy crowing at my brother John, his beloved eldest grandson, 'I'll match you over 100 yards when you're eighteen, boy! I'll walk down the aisle at your wedding!' All back from the grave, all home. Waves of laughter and tears crossing over.

But before that epiphany, if this was real life, there would be hours or days of preparation, negotiation, tension, not to mention shopping and bed-making and cooking, the rehearsing or erasing of half-forgotten fears and resentments, the burden of hope. Let everything be right, let everything be ready, what shall we tell them and not tell them? *Don't let us down.*

And after the perfect moment of reunion, what then?

I come from two different families, the Gees and the Churches. My parents' given names both tell a story. My father's was Victor Valentine Gee, quite a burdensome, aspirational one, expecting from the child who was born in 1914, the year the Great War broke out, exploits both martial and romantic. Vic was named for Valentine's Day, the day he was born on, a secret softness he tried to keep from the oikish adolescents he taught. His initials were V V G, which meant Very Very Good when teachers put it on homework; his demands on himself and others were high.

The Gees were clever and had standards, an end terrace house in Wolverton, Bucks, which meant they were upper working-class, a giant metal roller for the grass leaning against the garden wall, crimson hollyhocks six foot tall, and upstanding moral convictions. Wolverton was a grid of nearly identical red-brick terraced houses with blue slate roofs, a Victorian 'New Town' expressly built by the London and Birmingham Railway Company in 1838 to house the men who built the trains. Vic's father, my grandfather Walt, was a Labour man and trades union leader at 'The Works', supposedly a hero for turning down a large cash offer from the bosses to go over to management, a figure in the community, as he let me know one day: 'They'll never let me buy my own drinks, in the club,' he said with a wink. That didn't sound good to me. 'Why not?'

'The Club', the railway works pub-come-social club, was almost opposite number 72 Peel Road, and I associated it with happiness. Going up alone at night, since I was the youngest, to the dark first floor of my grandparents' Victorian house, creeping into my soft snow-cold feather-bed with its small warm heart, the stone hot

water-bottle put there in advance, I would wait shivering until the
music across the way began, and the hum of male voices; then the
light from the club, getting brighter as night fell, imprinted through
the curtain an intricate, impossibly beautiful, longed-for pattern
of lace on the wall.

Why couldn't Grandpa buy his own drinks? 'There's always
someone wants to buy me a drink,' he divulged, and offered me
another treacle toffee, a paper bag of which soft dark brown squares
he always kept in the pocket of his jacket 'to keep himself regular',
as Grandma explained, for pleasure in this ascetic family always
needed justifying, except for my grandfather's fondness for drink.
At tea (which was also supper) there was a clear rule, no jelly or fruit
cake without bread and butter.

Grandpa was a trim, fit man, with bristling white hair, kept short,
and a neat moustache to disguise what might have been a hare lip
but was actually damage he did himself as a young man in Cosgrove,
the canal-side village where he grew up, by diving from the bridge
into too-shallow water. 'Pa' (as both my parents called him) wore
collarless striped shirts and a buttoned, fitted grey waistcoat, always
smart, with a watch and watch-chain, which leads me to his special
skill as a watch-maker and mender, with a workshop in the garden
which was sacrosanct, next to the outside lavvy with its puzzling
neat squares of torn newspaper speared on a hook. He sat in his
workshop, visible through the open top of the split 'stable-door' he
had put on, peering down god-like through his monocle-like watch-
glass at the tiny gleaming mechanical galaxies of cog and spring
he had opened up. No one dared disturb him there, still less go in
and touch the minute spread pieces of metal that in my memory
would cover the whole of his work-top like hard glittering fallen
petals, infinitely interesting but forbidden. Once or twice he let
me look in, but always with a firm, 'Don't touch, my duck.' Did he
understand how I longed to, loving as I always did (and still do) the
detailed and microscopic? He made three grandfather clocks for his

three sons, the wooden cases slightly dull but the faces meticulously scrolled and furled and the hands like the elegant dark outlines of heads of herons.

Pa was also his chairs; where the rest of the family relaxed in armchairs or on the brown cracked leatherette sofa with its worn velvet cushions, Pa was only ever seen to sit perfectly erect in one of two upright wooden carver chairs he had made, one at the head of the table in the kitchen where we ate, one, with a pale blue-green-silver brocade slip-over cushion sewn by Grandma to soften the back, in the little dark sitting-room, semi-obstructing the door to the hall, an *en-garde* throne where no one but Grandpa ever dared to sit.

It was a family of men, one of those families genetically biased towards boys. My father was one of three brothers, three sons, Cecil, Victor and Lloyd, though my grandmother was said to have wanted a girl so much that she kept my father's blond locks long till he was five years old, thus causing him to be known as 'Mrs Gee's Fairy' – not easy, especially when you secretly know you have a cissy second name, Valentine. Only Lloyd achieved parity between the genders, with a boy and a girl, Martyn and Susan, who (miraculously) always seemed to get on. Cecil had one son, clever Keith, who produced three boys; Vic had me, of course, and I, very late but lucky, gave birth to a girl, but he also had two boys, my brothers John and James, who fathered six boys between them. I grew up very used to men.

Grandma Gee probably suffered from men, and certainly suffered from Pa, who was difficult. A lean, driving, impatient, intelligent man who had been a sprinter, and still walked, in old age, at a furious pace, despite his doctor warning him to slow down. He did so, on his morning walk, for the few yards of pavement that passed the doctor's surgery, then sped up to a military clip again, a little deception of which he often boasted. Grandma and Grandpa Gee's arguments were bad, and my father, who as a boy had always been drawn in on his mother's side, and still did, as an adult, get enmeshed in Oedipal fights against his father which made us children tremble, later decided that Pa had sometimes been right; perhaps because he saw himself in turn becoming Pa, with a manifestly suffering wife, and with children, my brother and me, who'd been turned against him. The first argument between my parents I remember was when I was six or seven, at Watersfield, when I came home from school for lunch. I think it was about food; why was my father at home? Was Mum's cooking not up to the occasion? I think she had cooked bubble-and-squeak, fried-up potatoes and cabbage, which was something the Church family ate and was actually one of my early childhood favourites; maybe it wasn't good enough for Dad, who had very recently become a headmaster, pulling himself up with pure determination by his own boot-straps; maybe he wanted food that spoke of their new bright future. What was terrible was seeing my mother cry at table, and my father saying, 'I have no respect for tears, Ma always used tears.'

Ma: Grandma Gee. The frailest of my four grandparents, dying relatively young, in her seventies.

Charlotte or Lottie Gee née Brown looked small and delicate (though plump, liking peppermint imperials 'for my digestion'), with a tiny nose, round cheeks, dimples I inherited and bright blue eyes. By the time I remember her, she had fine pleated pale skin, curled white hair and a chronically bad hip, as well as diabetes and Reynaud's disease – fingers and toes whose blood-vessels go into spasm with cold, turning whitish-blue, and when the blood-flow suddenly returns, an alarming reddish-purple (she died, in the end, from a heart attack followed by gangrene). She still loved clothes, particularly hats, and elaborately pin-tucked blouses worn with brooches over her big soft bosom, and was prone to tell me things I had never thought about, but liked, such as 'Yellow suits you'. Grandma made a pet of me, I think because Pa made a pet of my cousin Susan, the only other girl in my generation of Gees, daughter of Vic's brother Lloyd. Sue was very slightly younger than me, and much prettier, with the big blue family eyes (mine were green) and a perfect button nose (mine was long and Irish), and lived in Wolverton, thus having the advantage of playing for the home team. Sue had what seemed to me a huge wardrobe of wonderful dresses, because her mother Aunty Hilda, unlike my own beloved mother, was good at buying and making clothes. But Grandma, known to everyone but her grandchildren as Ma, took me into her bed as a treat in the mornings and whispered the unthinkable: 'Susan isn't prettier than you.' I must have asked her, or she wouldn't have said it. 'You'll be very pretty one day.' This was amazing; I was skinny, with glasses, but perhaps if Grandma said so it was true. (I have a vague uneasy memory of checking what Grandma had said with Grandpa. I really wanted to know: 'Am I prettier than Susan? Grandma says I am' – which was not exactly what she had said, but was what I hoped to hear. 'No, you're not.' Serves me right.)

Grandma made me pretty clothes. I was helped to be a girl by the extended family. My mother's deficiencies as a dress-maker must have been common knowledge, because everyone made me clothes, some of them remarkable: Grandma knitted me an outfit of multiple pieces in royal blue wool – (is blue royal any more? richer, deeper than sky-blue) – that had a short gathered skirt with buttoned over-the-shoulder straps, a beret, and a bibbed one-piece bathing suit. When I outgrew it she knitted me another bibbed swimsuit I liked even better, orange with a sharp white edge. Best of all, she made me a fluffy white angora bolero, softest, lightest, whitest delight. Aunty Ede, Ma's sister, who had worked in the cotton-mills in Leeds (was it my father who told me that the three sisters came south from Bradford?) sent a work of art when I had just started junior school, a wonderfully busy cardigan with eight large cats' faces, four on each side, knitted in relief, with green eyes and embroidered whiskers, and the neck and cuffs edged with knitted piecrust frills in scarlet, drawn in with scarlet threads finished with pom-poms. With what passion I wore it to school and accepted compliments (it must have dazzled, in the austere post-war world of the 1950s), how vividly it shines more than fifty years later from the phantom closets of my childhood. Aunty Elsie, on my mother's side, posted, about a year later, just before we moved to Watersfield, a dress of great beauty. Indeed the most beautiful dress I had ever seen: filmy white muslin with raised dots of pale blue, pale blue smocking across the bust, white Peter Pan collar decorated with palest blue 'S'-bending ric-rac braid, one row of it there and two on the hem, and puffed sleeves. Tragedy: it was too small (and my father was cross: I cried and insisted it fitted, as it strained and creaked under the arms, and he blamed Aunt Elsie because she was from my mother's side). Compensation: Elsie also sent a white satin petticoat, frilled, which was almost as pretty and fitted me perfectly, though I was never allowed to wear it on its own to birthday parties, as I wanted. When I was confirmed, yet another aunt, Bertha, my godmother, made me a white gathered skirt and blouson boat-necked top from a stiff heavy material that proclaimed my fourteen-year-old virtue (would any fourteen-year-old girl now living in Britain accept, sight unseen, a skirt and top sewn by her aunt?). But I wanted to like it, and did: on family windfalls rested my adolescent hopes of femininity and glamour.

There were reasons why my mother wasn't, at least while I was young, very good at getting me clothes. For a start, money. There can't have been much, when Dad was only a teacher and she (because he was a traditional man) wasn't working. Dad had said, in his very unromantic wartime proposal on the station platform when he was on leave from the Air Force, 'Two can live as cheaply as one, Aileen'; but three, and then four, and then five, as they added children, could not. All the same, the rest of the family, source of my extravagant gifts, were no richer, and most of them were poorer. It wasn't just money. Now I see it was because of my mother's own childhood. A seventh child and third daughter, Mum never had any new clothes of her own, only cast-offs. How was she to know how to make them, or what to buy?

And so we move to the Churches: my other family, my other side. My mother was Aileen Mary Church, but should have been Eileen. The C of E vicar objected to Eileen (because the name was Irish, thus possibly Popish. Zillah Meakins, Mum's grandma on her father's side, seems to have been Irish and probably what was then called a 'tinker', a gypsy; the Meakinses were frequently away, and had their children christened in batches.) The amiability with which her father changed tack at the christening when the vicar baulked was said to be down to drink, but it also tells you something about the gap between Gees and Churches, because it is inconceivable that a Gee would have changed the name of their child from Eileen to Aileen on a vicar's, or anyone's, say-so – not when they were sober and even less when drunk.

Gees, I was always hearing, had 'character' and 'backbone'. 'If you're going to do a thing, do it right.' 'Stick to your guns.' I see these traits come down into Walt Gee's grandchildren, ourselves and our Gee cousins: dogged determination, self-belief, drive, competitiveness at sport and life, on the plus side tenacious loyalty and a mission to do something good in the world, on the minus – I see it in myself – a tendency to be sanctimonious, and at our worst, grandiose. Lucky for me then, lucky for my husband and daughter and friends, that my brothers and I are half my mother's, touched with the redeeming brush, I hope, of the supple, easy-going, anarchic, witty, unashamedly self-interested, sensual, unsentimental, potentially criminal Churches.

Aileen's family lived in Stony Stratford, a walk away across the fields from Wolverton, in a smaller terraced house on London Road facing the graveyard, which had two rooms downstairs, the back room where we sat and ate and the front room for best, never used, with a scullery out at the back and an outside loo that was a wooden plank with a round hole in it over darkness, and smelled. They were not, like the Gees, upper working-class; Mum said the Gees were 'a cut above'. The Churches were lower working-class, and mostly

Tories, which went against their own class interest, whereas Gees, being argumentative, were Labour. I imagine the Churches found Labour politicians too smug for their taste.

When Mum was small, she remembered the family being so poor that her mother had to cut fried eggs in two. She had contracted TB, which flourishes in overcrowded conditions like theirs, but recovered. Grandpa Church, Bill Church, had been in the Indian Army in the First World War, where he was a non-commissioned officer in the mess, and had such a good time – (there is a group photograph in which he is the only man wearing his cap pushed right back on his head, showing thick black curls, and a big unmilitary, sarky, sociable smile) – that he didn't want to come home. Then Bill worked as a smelter in the steel works, a hellishly thirsty job requiring a lot of beer in the pub on Sunday morning, after which he returned a different man for his lunch, surly and furious, and my mother and Aunty Eve hid under the table.

But by the time I remember him Grandpa Church was an old man, rheumy-eyed, flushed, immensely genial, small and rather loose-lipped, his longish white hair covered now by a beige flat cap, in a brown cardigan, who did a pensioner's part-time job in a grocer's shop, and made jokes about giving us a ride on the bacon-slicer, which, not understanding, I was eager to accept. Grandma Church had been a 'help' for Mrs Coe, not far away in the same row of terraced houses, all of which the Coes owned, doing her washing and cleaning, and must have cleaned for others too. May Church had had seven children (though she lost one, a little boy called Louis, possibly from the TB which my mother survived), making my own mother Aileen, the youngest, that magical thing, the 'seventh of a seventh of a seventh', the third-generation child who supposedly has premonitions, 'the sight'.

Did she? My mother was reluctant to give up that reputation, rationalist though at bottom she was, saying her premonitions were 'always bad'. (But I think of her, *au fond*, as an optimist, a woman who lived in the cheerful, accepting, make-the-most-of-it present, whereas my insistently upbeat father – 'Never look back', 'Don't talk about death', and on the telephone later, demanding a 'Yes', 'Are you fit and well?' – was at bottom more fearful than her, an ingenious, comprehensive worrier.)

Gees, descendants of the perfectionist craftsman and activist, Pa, and the needlewoman and aspirational homemaker, Ma, who hung framed reproductions of pictures like Watts's *Blind Hope* on the sitting-room wall and had a four-shelf bookcase of mostly improving books, became craftsmen or teachers themselves, jobs with a certain rectitude. My elder brother John became head teacher of a comprehensive school, like our father; my younger brother Jim began, and ran, the NHS Counter Fraud Service; I am a moralising writer (though my anarchic side is pure Church). How proud Grandpa and Grandma Gee would have been! Churches, the more numerous offspring of slapdash Bill Church and fey May Davis (of whom it was said, by a possibly jealous sister-in-law, 'she couldn't even make a decent cup of tea'), had more dubious skills. One of Mum's brothers was a bookie's runner, one did conjuring tricks, all told jokes (Gees couldn't) and were slightly cynical and made each other laugh, one was photographed smiling in an elegantly laid-back way near the top of a human pyramid, some emigrated, all liked money even if they had none, and some, like Eve and Albert, managed to acquire it. Churches occasionally had illegitimate babies, Gees had lifelong but not always amicable marriages. Churches had a gene, usually suppressed but life-enhancing, for red hair, as expressed in the waves of my beautiful, rebellious and eventually well-off cousin Maureen, and the crimson crest (heightened with henna) of my purple-and-turquoise-wearing, cricket- and claret-loving, scientific, artistic and eccentric second cousin Jane Teather; Mum had some chestnut in her thick dark hair, and my daughter Rosa was a strawberry blonde until she was six. Red meant, well, a bit raffish. Where Gees became trades unionists and in later generations lefties, Churches became Foresters or freemasons, liking the secrecy, the drink and the dinners. Uncle Albert was a Worshipful Master and once, vowing me to secrecy, showed me his gilt and silver regalia, which in my memory (but can this be right?) included an elaborate garter; his wife Aunt Eve, my mother's sister, wore furs, had enormous gold rings on all her arthritic fingers, collected silver Masonic gifts, and drew in her eyebrows half an inch above the ghost of her real ones. They were snobs, and gossips, though kind and generous, and my father suspected them of patronising him. Churches had charm in bucketfuls, Gees had pride in spades.

When my mother was dying in hospital (because, as happens so often, death suddenly bore down before we could get her out) and the morphine was carrying her a little away from herself, she slipped back into the past, and talked about the churchyard opposite the house where she was born: 'There are women in long white dresses walking about between the graves,' she told me as I sat by her bedside. One sentence she repeated, holding my hand: 'There's someone waiting for me at home who is good as gold, good as gold.' This was her mother May, née May Davis, source of my mother's occasional feyness, genetic wellspring, I imagine, of my own writing, lover of rhymes, daughter of the nearest thing in my own family to a writer.

I only remember my mother's mother as a very old lady. Grandma Church was in her eighties when she died, in what must have been 1952, because I was only four and recall for some reason the gaiters and brown checked coat I wore on the day of her death, alas the same day as the death of one of the two spinster Gardiner sisters who lived next door, Miss Lou and Miss Grace. So that I, hopping in from the garden into the kitchen where my mother was crying, still chanting my repeated refrain of the day, 'Poor Grandma, poor Miss Gardiner,' was rounded on with natural asperity by my mother, who said, 'Never mind Miss Gardiner, how about *Grandma*?' – and my father made everything worse by telling her off for being unfair.

The guilt of having caused my mother double pain still gives me a little stab of unhappiness.

Grandma Church, to me, was an old lady, tall and big for an old lady, who made puzzling jokes and had long ashen and brindled hair wound around her head in a thin coiled sausage, and dark brown tortoise-shell spectacles. She had a fur coat with shiny worn edges that probably came from her employer Mrs Coe, but she still had a smiley mouth, not like the thin lips that most old people had, a feature I always admired in my mother, whose mouth never grew mean or old. Grandma Church would bend over and talk to me, so I liked her even if I never quite understood her, but then children never quite understand grownups, so this seemed nothing remarkable. I remember, one time when Grandma and Grandpa were staying with us at Bromsgrove, a conversation one day on the sunny landing about a hair, which Grandma showed me, and stroked across the palm of my hand (was it growing on her face? Perhaps.) When I reported this to my parents I recall my father looking serious, and saying something to my mother, who said, 'Oh she's all right, Vic, never mind.' This was explained much later when Mum told me that her mother had been 'senile' in her last few years but that Grandpa hadn't helped by 'taking over everything at home so she felt that she couldn't do anything at all'.

But what little my Mum also told me made it clear that her mother could have done anything if she had not been born poor. For a start, in the wedding photograph for her marriage to Bill Church, May Davis is strikingly beautiful, by far the best-looking of all the sisters and aunts in attendance, with big dreamy heavy-lidded eyes, full lips, only half-smiling, a small tip-tilted nose and pale blonde hair. Beside her Bill looks swarthy and sensual and Italianate or Jewish, and a little small. The secret of their marriage may have been that she was five years older than him, and thus almost on the shelf. Well, he gave her seven children, and to look at him, sex and laughs. It was May who read to my mother, and made her love books. And

Hat competition at the wedding of my maternal grandparents, Bill and May Church

this is the puzzle about the Davis side of the family: where did the education come from? Was there money, once, that was lost? Did it trickle away between all those sevenths of sevenths?

Because May's mother Martha Davis née Leeson, my great-grandma, was a poet of sorts, a strange, sharp-looking woman with a long curving crest of nose, thin witty lips and eyes set so wide they were practically looking in different directions. Fleshy in her middle years, corseted in black with a strict high neck and lace cap, in old age she attained a kind of hawk-like beauty – there is a faded photograph of her in glory, slender once more, mounted straight-backed and imperious on a tall machine which, Aunty Eve assured me, was 'the first tricycle in Northampton'. Did the money to acquire this style and dash come partly from writing?

Martha Leeson wrote verses for birthday and Christmas cards, in bulk, and took them to Market Harborough station in a suitcase, where she met a man who paid her, very little I imagine, and

Great-grandma Martha Davis née Leeson, writer of birthday-card verses

took them away. Is rhyme a genetic trick, an echo-receptive angle of the genome, I wonder? My mother could rhyme as easily as breathing, firing off her poems to women's magazines and winning ten shillings or the 'star letter spot' with regularity, and I find it hard not to rhyme when I write prose, and my daughter finds it natural to rap.

Grandma Church's stubbornness changed my mother's whole life for the better. Mum was born with a turned-in foot, and May her mother was told by the doctor that she would have to have a caliper; nothing could be done; little Aileen, her seventh child, would always walk with a limp. But May refused to accept it. Instead she carried my mother to and from the nearest hospital every week for treatment, 'three or four miles', as mum told me, and another three or four back. It worked; my mother later became a sprinter, hurdler and hockey-player, and I still have the small blackened silver cup that pronounces her Wolverton Grammar School Sports Day's 'victrix ludorum'.

In other ways Grandma Church had grown tired by the time my mother was born, after all those children, with no money and a husband who drank. That's probably why she didn't teach my mother how to sew, or make clothes, because Mum's elder sisters both had these skills. It must also be why, as my mother told me still with some sadness a lifetime later, 'Mum never came to any of my school events,' so Aileen had to shine on sports days unregarded (but she always came to everything that I did, by way of compensation; every play, every parents' evening, every Sports Day, there Mum would be, with a camera, smiling and cheering me on).

The battle between my parents – who nevertheless loved each other, and all of us – was fought through their families, as marital battles so often are. Gees were martial, while Churches appeased and then secretly deceived. My father was frightening and sometimes aggressive and my mother wasn't, and 'a man should lead', as he asserted, so when conflict was overt, he would always carry the day. When we made our regular visits 'home' to Bucks, the division of time was never just. We always stayed at Wolverton, with Pa and Ma, and only walked over the fields to my mother's home, Stony Stratford, for occasional meals. There my father felt off his ground, and uneasy, particularly, as I think now, after Grandma Church died, when there was just Grandpa Church to deal with, the man who my mother called 'Dad', the only plausible other man and authority figure in her life. Though Bill, shambling and laughing in his cardigan and slippers, with mould in his bread-bin and his tribe of seven children dispersed to the four winds, was far from being an authority figure. But he could annoy my father terribly, by making jokes and being funny, and once, I remember, just by saying, 'Relax, Vic, make yourself at home,' then going into the kitchen to prepare whatever we were eating, ham and pickled onions, probably, on thick plates, and by the time he returned my father had worked himself into a rage, fulminating to my mother, 'I AM relaxed, I AM at home, what does he mean?'

Of course my mother minded all this very much. And then, Vic criticised her brothers and sisters, when we were back in our own home and away from the battleground of Wolverton v. Stony Stratford. Eve and Albert were too rich and 'too selfish to have children' (which was far from being the case. I only understood how much sadness had been concealed when I was eighteen, and in a moment of revelation, Eve showed me, one day, the life-size blonde figure of a child, a giant doll over four feet tall, which she kept sitting on the sofa, when no one was there. She had called her Annabel. Was that selfish?) Arthur and Frances, also childless and therefore fond of their nieces and nephews, annoyed Dad by generously buying me, in the face of his protests, from Woolworths, the flat gold and silver cardboard crowns I craved, to celebrate the Coronation in 1953; I still remember the row between the grownups afterwards in the hot sunlight on Bromsgrove High Street, the horror of it, my gift poisoned with guilt, wishing I had not asked for it ... Uncle Arthur and Aunty Frances never came to stay again.

As I remember these quarrels I find myself growing annoyed with my father, for all the trouble he caused, for the gnawing anxiety under my ribs (it's there now) that I always had to feel, as a child, when we were going to family, 'to see people', or indeed going out at all, because visiting a café for a cup of tea or coffee was a minefield with my father – the staff might ignore or insult him, or other customers might sit too close, for he had an exaggerated sense of personal space, which must not be invaded or even passed through by others. This extended to houses and gardens (Vic needed to be detached, but could not afford it), and even to roads,

whether semi-private (on the little modern estate where they died
in a thin-walled, thin-skinned modern bungalow, he objected to
his neighbours' children riding their bikes down the shared access
road which passed his front window) or public (he drove very fast
and increasingly badly, and saw any overtaking as a challenge, so
it was normal to be roaring down the flat Norfolk roads with Dad
in a desperate race for pre-eminence, two abreast, his passengers
fearing death. The armour-plated Landrover they bought in their
fifties overturned at least twice and frequently disappeared for
repairs after crashes Dad never admitted to.)

Dad was a self-deluder, as all of us are, only more so. Not always,
and not at the end, when he faced the impossible thing he had always
rejected and fled, his death, with clear eyes, and courage. But the high
moral code he had been force-fed sometimes made him absurd: 'I
have never told a lie,' he would say, quite frequently, when accusing
one or other of us of untruth (thus telling a lie, of course). When
my brother and I got older, we questioned him: 'You must have
done, Dad.' 'No, never.' Shaking his head at us and himself to make
it true. He was never wrong, either; evidence was nothing to him,
he would simply refuse to consider it; some of the worst father-son
arguments of my elder brother's teenage years were about facts. For
example, about the time of a radio programme: John would leave the
room and reappear red-faced and triumphant pointing to the item
in the *Radio Times*, but my father, outraged, would shout, 'Leave
it!' and refuse to look.

As Gees go, Vic was acknowledged, even by other Gees, to be
an extreme example. My brothers, in my memory, though they
might say different, admired him more as their distance from home
lengthened. Male Gees have testosterone in buckets, or maybe that
should be spades: buckets AND spades. It is hard for a lot of male
Gees to fit into a tiny house, especially when one or more of them
is adolescent.

But it was my father, really, who never grew up, not his sons.

Part of Dad remained an inconsolable child, needing to be loved and praised more than anyone I have ever known, horribly easily thrown off kilter emotionally, for all his jut-jawed determination. He imagined the world wanted to fight with him, to put him down. He fought back relentlessly, but it cost him. He had to rehearse whatever had happened with my mother, over and over, until she was exhausted. He could never let anything drop until she had acknowledged him to be entirely in the right. Of course: with such a fragile ego, how could he afford to be wrong? How bored she must have been, how tired, and her 'Yes Vic's would become thinner and thinner, her face blank, her voice hoarsened by suppressed irritation and disbelief.

(But then, wives should tell their husbands the truth at least some of the time. If only she could have been braver at the beginning, when all habits are made. Wives have to let their husbands know the reality of how they are behaving in the world, as husbands should wives, since that is part of the compact of marriage: *I will help you understand how others see you.* My mother got too tired and too frightened to keep that part of the bargain.)

Since one of my aims in this book is to try to find a way to forgiveness, of others as well as myself, I have to ask why Vic was ill-at-ease enough to make others around him so uneasy. Never at home enough unless literally in his own home, and even then, in old age he started to keep the curtains half-closed so people couldn't look in. Partly, once again, I would put this down to fundamental differences in the geography of Gees and Churches. The Churches managed to live, nine-strong, in a house with barely half a dozen rooms, in a row where a common path ran all along the back to link the whole terrace. Their back step down to the path was less than ten feet away from the next back step where their neighbours sat, and the long strips of garden were not divided by fences. It all spoke of easy communal and social life, contact with the outside world, relatively low expectations. The Gees, by contrast, five-strong, lived in an end-terrace house twice as big. Their garden – end-terrace houses always had bigger gardens, which partly accounted for their status – was firmly enclosed by a tall red-brick wall with a pointed rooflet of blue slate. No one called at the front, and to get to the back door from the criss-cross of 'back ways', like northern back ways, you had to mount a big step and press a noisy metal latch to open the gate, then traverse the blue-grey path through the garden. Pa's home was his castle; so, later, to our detriment, was Vic's.

And then there was the year Vic was born, that ominous 1914. He was six months old when the archduke's nephew was assassinated at Sarajevo, starting the great war that fed the soil of Europe with the blood and bones of frightened young male humans. Grandma Gee was already pregnant again, with Lloyd, too soon for my father, who was always jealous of his younger brother, born before my father was one, taking Ma's love and attention. Meanwhile Grandma Gee's own two beloved brothers, Joe and William (known as 'Laddie'), the only boys on the Brown side of the family, had gone off as private soldiers with the Oxford and Bucks Light Infantry. And thus began the tragedy whose aftermath Grandma whispered to me one morning, tucked up in her bed in the downstairs front room, for by then she was too frail to go upstairs, and I remember it soft and warm, a nest of talc and lace and specialness (for she was telling me secrets) and safety; safe because I didn't really understand what she said. How can you understand death before anyone close enough to be painfully missed has died? How was I to know why the beautiful photo of frail soft Grandma as a young married woman, centre of a triptych of sisters, showed her in elaborate black silk, with a huge black feathered hat, and behind the girls their mother, Mrs Brown, toothless and grim with a great dark mourning plume bursting out of her head like black smoke?

One died in Salonika, one in France. Grandma told me how she and her sister Kit had 'gone to look for the graves of your great-uncles –'. 'Which uncles?' 'You never knew them, pet.' She and Kit

Left to right, front: Kit, Lottie (my paternal grandma) and Ede, after the death of both their brothers, with Great-grandma Brown behind

'had never been abroad before, we didn't speak any French, but we were determined to find them.' What she told me was comedy: not speaking any French, she and Kit had 'needed to go to the lav', 'So we had to get down and squat, to show them! Squattay Voo!' I loved this story, which gave me a completely different idea of my invalid grandma, as an intrepid explorer (and indeed that was part of the truth that time had obscured, for my own mother told me that Ma, when young, used to take her sons on the train up to London, which made Vic's inability to let Mum go out on her own seem especially puzzling).

It isn't, though, when I think. His need for her was limitless. Behind Ma's story were the deaths of the only men in her family, both of them killed before Dad was three (and my father once told me, with tears in his eyes, that Laddie said to Ma he was 'going off to fight for me', for the baby who was born just before the war started; Laddie fought, and died; did the legend of his sacrifice leave Dad feeling guilty?). How much grief and mourning was there in my father's early years, how much terror between the deaths of the first young uncle and the second? How did Ma, in her sorrow, manage to look after her sensitive son, 'Grandma Gee's Fairy?'

Maybe that was why she wanted him to be a girl: so he wouldn't have to go off and be killed, like her brothers.

It all left my father with a horror of death and funerals. Children must be protected from death: 'Never look back' was his watchword; we didn't attend our grandparents' funerals, nor the uncles' and aunts'. I realise now that the first family funeral I ever attended was my own father's. By then I was in my forties. Being dead, Dad couldn't stop me going. He would never consider insuring his life, refused to take anything from the house when his parents died except one photograph of Aunt Ede 'for Margaret', and was so averse to contemplating his own death that his pension stopped with him, leaving my mother, in the end, with no income. There had been a lifetime of relative comfort for which she always thanked him, and made us be thankful too, saying, 'Your dad is a good provider', because she remembered, from childhood, real poverty, and loved, in the 1980s, getting cash from the wall. But because of Dad's phobia about death, in 1992 she was left with almost nothing.

Not for long. She had cared for him tenderly, if not ungrudgingly, maybe as his grieving mother never could, over the last five years when he was blind and had Parkinson's disease. Life gave him a second chance at being helpless and receiving love, fulfilling the infant need that was thwarted by the precipitate arrival of his brother. Till death us do part: he needed, and Mum supplied.

No one is fixed and nothing is forever. One day, when I had a family of my own, as my father and I walked up the garden path, single file, Dad going ahead, he was nearly at the door and he said 'Sorry' to me. 'Sorry for the things I did wrong. Whatever I did wrong. When you were younger. I know I did.' I was taken by surprise, and mortified later that all I managed was instinctively to comfort him, as my mother had shown me men should be comforted: 'Never mind, Dad, it's all right.'

Which was not, perhaps, enough; I was genuinely grateful, but part of me felt ambushed, as if I should at least have had a chance to say, 'Yes, you did wrong.' But now I see that his apology was difficult, and brave. And that all those family wars were just something he could not avoid. Raging did not make him happier, though it made us less happy; my father could do no other. He struck out when words weren't sufficient to express the hurt or injustice he felt, the outraged unfairness; *why didn't we love him enough, why didn't we support him, why did we undermine and defy him?*

With a different wife, not a seventh of a seventh of a seventh with her damaged sense of self coming down through three generations, with a woman who stood up to him openly, rather than deferring, as Mum did, until she had no more ground to concede, all the while subverting his children with her charm and sweetness, and isolating him – could Dad have been different? Maybe. As it was, Victor couldn't win.

Scissors, paper, stone: that elemental children's game. The Gees were scissors who cut through things, and obdurate stone which resisted. The charming Churches were paper, having the last word in secret, enfolding and circumventing, camouflaging, wrapping things up for a party, making life fun.

And in later life, when the two elder children had gone, when the mortgage was paid off and the head teacher's inflation-linked pension finally arrived and made their life comfortable, Aileen solved the great puzzle of clothes, those coded rags that claim status or artistry or beauty, saying 'I am here, look at me.' For herself, she bought layers of gypsy-like colour that made her look not unlike my dark-haired, long-tressed great-grandmother Zillah Meakins, reds and purples, waistcoats and scarves, and grew her hair, still thick and wavy in her seventies, down to her shoulders. For her children and grandchildren, by a sudden miraculous sleight of hand, she also provided clothes, doing in old age what she couldn't manage as a young mother. She started knitting, with flamboyance, imagination, and steadily increasing skill, Ziggy Stardust tank-tops of her own design for myself and my younger brother, mixing black with silver and gold and crimson. One extravagant top, a kind of evening waistcoat, gold-buttoned, she dreamed up entirely from gleaming metallic thread, with elaborate Fair Isle patterns on the front woven from silver and gold, a pale shining wisp that clung lightly to my waist and breasts, like nothing else, un-sensible, fabulously sinuous, charm itself. As if all those years there had been orchids of gilded sartorial sensuousness rooting themselves in the dark deep down in Mum's psyche, waiting only for the sunlight of money and time to break free. I wore that shimmering garment to parties for years, and now it belongs to my twenty-two-year-old daughter, Rosa, who wears, unmistakably, also, the witty, rebellious, unputdownable, charming smile of the Churches; tells jokes and does imitations like a Church, and, mostly, lets things go.

So which side won?

Alas, neither side won. In struggles between two families, no one can win. I just wish they had learned to get on. After all, the two strains continue now, intertwined. I adored my mother, but my father's determination and eye for detail hold me in their pinions still, never leaving me alone; holding me up, driving me on.

4 My animal luck (ii)

I am born:
and make my father jealous

I began early, long and white and premature and so sleepy that my parents feared I was 'not quite right': did nothing but drink milk. They worked my arms and legs in swimming motions, trying to reassure themselves. My mother Aileen looks thin and dark and fierce in the photographs, for she was not well after I was born, but she clutches me to her, and her eyes are bright. She said that this thirty-third year of her life was her happiest; she loved her son John but now she wanted a daughter.

That morning Mum had walked with my father into Poole, by the sea, to pick up an orange roll of stair-carpet for Tatnam Road, because the in-laws were expected. November 2nd: blowing leaves, squalling seagulls. My parents-to-be marched back through the wind carrying the roll of carpet, taking one end each, her bump sticking out from her thinness, stopping every now and again for John, aged three and a half, to catch up. Tea was cucumber sandwiches, and I arrived in a hurry two hours later. That rush birth was good for my mother but left a little mark on me. One of my only two recurrent dreams is of knowing I have to shoot down a long narrow tunnel to save my life and get into the light, and in the dream I can never do it, there is a half-formed dream thought that death would be better, but in a refusal of death, I wake up. Maybe one day when death becomes physically real I will be brave enough to dream my way through this dark tunnel and find whatever life is at the other end.

Loving life as I do, I would like to have another one, to go on trying to understand. But my rational mind thinks, with regret, that there must be an infinite variety of souls or selfhoods, as there is an endless serendipity of currents on the sea; why should one soul be reused? (And another voice, holding to belief, says, 'Nothing in the world disappears. Mass becomes energy, heat becomes light, bones are made from stardust, ash feeds the roses.' Why should the tiny detailed net of tensile electrical connectivity that is a single consciousness be lost?)

The first voice answers, we have to make room. There has to be space for the not-yet-born, for becoming, or the system would be dead and closed. Our 'once-ness' makes us, and the world, and love, more precious.

It will just be hard to say goodbye, one day. Harder than the headlong fearful rush down the dark tunnel that brought me – a six-pound mewling animal, skinny, half-blinded by the light, shining with womb-grease, mother-naked, sucking up air as I woke – into this radiant, temporary room.

I was born in 1948, three years after the end of the war, during which my father Victor (always Vic) had been a meteorologist in the Air Force, posted in India and Iceland. He had said to my mother, as fathers say when they are in love, 'I want a little girl just like you.' What he got, in fact, was a reverse image; I was as pale as my mother was dark and vibrant; I had lint-white fine hair and she had thick black waves; her skin was olive, mine, as a child, transparent. (But thirty-eight years later, by the long-distance mathematics of genes, my own daughter would be born, blonde like me but with curls, lips, cheeks, eyes like my mother's: the 'little girl just like you'.)

There was still rationing, I think until I was about four or five

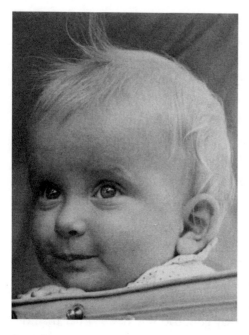

I was born in 1948

years old, because I remember red stamps in a grey book, and picking up orange juice from a Nissen hut. And the excitement of Grandpa Church, my mother's father, producing a pineapple as a present, when I was at infants' school. I recorded this in my diary, and the teacher unwisely wrote in pencil, 'Where did he get it?' I reflected on my grandfather's life and added, 'He got it down the pub,' which made my mother indignant.

That is the age when everything you know, you know without doubt, even when it is completely wrong. 'Idiot' was pronounced 'eye-dot', because that was the way I first read it to myself. I told my father, with great conviction, that Uncle Stan had come to visit my mother, indeed I still seem to remember seeing dark-haired, skinny, smiling Uncle Stan, husband of my mother's beautiful sister Alice, coming to the back door of our Victorian semi in Bromsgrove, and being welcomed with a shout of pleasure from my mother. But Uncle Stan had never been to Bromsgrove, and did not look as I described him either, so my story about the 'uncle' put my father in a jealous rage. I had 'too much imagination', of course, and everything I clearly imagined, I believed to be true.

At night this produced both excitements and horrors. Like many children and few adults, I 'saw' things on the darkness, clear and vivid, with my eyes open; to science it's a known phenomenon, 'eidetic imagery'. They were real and bright as day; historical pageants, in which I was somehow a part, having lived before (as I believed until I was well into my teens), turreted Disneyesque castles outlined against technicolour cloudscapes, heroic adventures my brother and I marched away on. Sometimes however the visions went wrong. I would see the chain-link fences that were everywhere then, around institutions like schools, grey links of metal in rounded-off diamonds supported by rusting struts, and one night my room was so chokingly full of it, marching down on me from every wall, that I called my mother in a panic.

She must have been tired, or my father was in a bad mood, because the one who arrived, with her back to the lit-up landing, black against the light, was the other mother I clearly knew also existed, not my loving, gentle mother but her doppelgänger, angry and slightly hoarse. I told her about the chain mail, which she could not see although it was everywhere. She tried to be kind, and was kind, looking round the world she could see for any evidence of fencing, and finally came up with some dark braid dangling from the edge of the round papyrus lampshade above my bed. I thought, 'This is hopeless,' and then *I* was kind. Because I saw that she needed to go, and she could not help me; and in any case, she had come, and the landing light made my room less frightening, more finite, and me less afraid, so I pretended the braid was the only problem, and she fetched some scissors and cut the ends off, then went away leaving the landing light on and the door half-open and myself only half-alone, and at least half-comforted. Because as long as love tries, it is love, though we all live in different worlds. If love is the urge behind the act, then surely there are no objective failures? And to think you are loved enough – to list, sometimes, the names of those who have loved you and who you love, without drawing up more demanding accounts of profit and loss – is for me the beginning of happiness.

5 I am in print

instead of Jane

Print arrived, as an extension of myself, when I was seven or eight. For today's children with their keyboards and computers and printers, there's nothing magic about it. But print, in the 1950s, was something removed from the sphere of childhood, something professional and grownup. To me it became an obsessive excitement.

Children like me learned to write in pencil, with unsatisfying slowness. I was hard on myself about writing; I liked to write my name in all my books, but then only months later would go back and be appalled by the crippled 'M' like a collapsing mountain range, the big straggly 'A' with its tepee-like overgrowth at the top, the 'R' like a rudimentary bird, the 'g' in 'Margaret' a sudden lower-case, humble and loopy, scraping the bottom of the barrel of my name, the uneven capital letters of 'GEE' in a drunken final dance, with 'E's like broken forks. I rubbed out and rewrote so many times that the frontispieces of my books were worn bare.

Why was I so harsh? It's true that, in different ways, both my parents were perfectionists, a trait which imprints itself without fail on the children in letters of fire. But I remember my mother protesting at the time and saying, 'That writing was very good for your age, leave it alone.' I refused to stop rubbing, worrying a blurry grey hole in the page. More likely this habit went back to my first day at the Bromsgrove, Worcestershire, infants' school, when a teacher whose name I don't remember gave us all strips of pale

cardboard with our names on to copy into books, and instead I wrote
down, triumphant, the name as my mother had taught it me, big, in
capitals, MARGARET MARY GEE: which was roundly rejected
by my teacher, who told me, 'We don't write in capitals now we are
at school,' took my paper away and made me do it again like the
cardboard strip, correctly. I went home ashamed and infused with
scorn for myself and my mother, though of course, as any parent
will know, big letters are easier to write with their straight lines and
right-angles. But they weren't on the teacher's card.

This was the start of a troubled relationship to writing by hand
that lasted until I was in my mid-teens. Too deferential on that first
day, too critical later of my own first tries, I became in time a guerrilla
warrior of handwriting. We seemed always to be moving schools (I
went to three different primary schools as my family moved from
Worcestershire to Sussex) and at each fresh school, I had the secret
advantage of knowing, as the new teacher did not, what I had been
taught before. The first time I moved, to tiny Watersfield village
school where all the juniors sat in one room, divided by age into rows,
I said, with perfect honesty, that I had been taught at Bromsgrove
to write in loops, and found to my surprise I was allowed to keep
them, in the face of Roman-nosed Mr Norris's preferred italics. In
any case it didn't really matter how I wrote, since I could not in any
respect learn to handle the new school's white china ink-pots, full of
made-up lumpy ink, that slotted into holes in the rows of desks, nor
the stained wooden dip-pens with their tortured and twisted metal
beaks, some crossed, which spluttered and creaked on our exercise
books. I was ink all over: hands, face, books, skirt.

Came the day of the visitor from somewhere outside in a
mackintosh – maybe London? I was only six – and the whole school
gathered together to watch an inspiring slide-show, on a hanging
screen, about Typhoo tea. We saw pictures of glowing green India,
and women in beautifully patterned pinks and reds, their heads
protected by scarves, picking 'only the finest tips' from the rows

of tea-plants. We were told a little about the women's lives, and a lot about the life-story of the tea, how it shrank black and dry and arrived at last in silver-paper packets cased in small neat cardboard boxes, to be decanted into the metal caddies on all our mothers' kitchen-shelves. (British kitchens, like Indian tea-picking jobs, then belonged only to the mothers.) The opening of this window on the world by the raincoated visitor from London presaged a great excitement: the Typhoo Tea Handwriting Competition.

The assembled school was instructed by Mr Norris to write the story of a day in the life of a tea-picker, for possible 'national prizes'. Alight with the happiness of ignorant invention, I wrote a five-page, semi-illegible saga of the life of a woman to whom I gave the well-known Indian name of Iris. Mr Norris saw past the ink-storm and was delighted; he read out my essay to the whole school, all twenty or so of us, that is, including the 'top class', a row by the window of six giant boys with big legs in short trousers who looked at me sourly. Three stories were submitted for the overall Typhoo prize, including mine, which I hoped was the best. All three stories came back unplaced in the overall competition, but with consolation 'school' prizes; big-legged Roy from the 'top class' was, I think, first, Margaret Gee third. Typhoo clearly took the handwriting aspect of the competition more seriously than Mr Norris; they must have been puzzled by my submission with its shambling, no-longer-tutored, ink-spurting loops.

At my next berth, Billingshurst County Primary, which also taught italic, I hung on grimly to my loops, swearing that this was what Watersfield had taught me; and at Horsham High School I was one of the only loop-writers in my year. But then around fifteen, when all pressure was past, I decided, like every adolescent, to design my own signature, and at the same time to revamp my handwriting. Italics were suddenly the only stylish choice; loops now seemed slow and fusty. I have been an italic writer ever since, and, too late for the Typhoo Tea prize, am legible and neat.

But quite early into this story of manual strain and difficulty, print erupted, objective, grownup, an amazement.

Machines in the 1950s tended to be clunky and cabinet-sized, of public interest. They arrived in town centres or on railway stations, to be admired and inspected. Our most regular journeys as a family were back from Bromsgrove, or later Billingshurst, to Wolverton, and on one such journey, changing as we did in London but also from time to time at stations like Crewe, all four of us were impressed by a giant crimson machine on the station platform.

What it ejected (primed with money and the right manipulations of a heavy-duty handle on the right, a thing like the massive hand of a clock which could be pointed, creaking, to various letters) was slim strips of soft metal, like gardeners' plant labels, aluminium or more likely lead, I think now, on which anything you chose could be printed in relief, standing up in glorious regularity, part of the public world, indubitable, beyond the reach of carping by teachers, safe from my own desperate efforts with erasers, definitely true: MARGARET GEE.

It was, like the advent of the typewriter early in the twentieth century and the computer and printer of the last two decades, part of the second phase of the Gutenberg revolution, in which print became commonplace, democratic. In the first, fifteenth-century, phase, the invention of print took writing and reading beyond the constraints of the careful caste of monks who copied books by hand. But printing was still laborious, controlled by the small number of printing-presses and the beliefs and tastes of those who owned them. Books remained relatively few, expensive and respected. Now in the twenty-first century the meaning of print has changed: it has lost perhaps half its authority for that half of the world who have it at their fingertips. Few people with a printer in their bedroom and advertising copy spewing through their letter-boxes will believe something just because it is printed.

In 1955 things were different. Books were still valued partly because of the war, ended only a decade ago, when paper was rare and publishers put, apologetically, 'war economy standard' in the front of their books, to show that production was under constraint. Typewriters were massive iron things, black-painted upright sisters of sewing-machines, more for offices than private houses. The success of italic writing depended partly on its clarity and its resemblance to type, the way it brought individual writing closer to the public sphere, moving in the opposite direction to the extravagant loops and coils of eighteenth- and nineteenth-century copperplate which had tilted it towards luxury, privacy, eccentricity.

There was a brief phase, during which I myself grew up, when ordinary names like mine could gain awesome stature and authority by being printed, thanks to machines like my railside crimson mammoth and all the other different kinds of personalised printing that followed – black plastic strips with white raised letters, transparent sheets of fragile 'Letraset' transfer letters, machine-embroidered cloth name-tapes, ordered through the post, that magically produced multiple perfect 'Margaret Gees'.

With my new metal printed strips from the station, I was almost famous. I was real. I had somehow joined the world of books, or had proved I could join, one day, the world of books. I think the day when I came home with my laboriously stamped-out name on grey metal clutched in the pocket of my duffel-coat, and found, almost unbelieving, that it was still there next day and was not a dream, was even more exciting than the day two or three years later when *Mickey Mouse* comic's 'News' page carried a medium-sized headline half-way down, ranged left: 'BUDDING AUTHORESS OF BILLINGSHURST, AGED 10.'

To my brother's amazement *Mickey Mouse* reported that the B A of B, Margaret Gee, had sent in a 'book' about a cowboy ranch. It was true. I had written it by hand, in blue ink, twenty pages of Basildon Bond (the small size, also blue), its own glued-pad-formation reinforced with sellotape. The book had changed course half-way through, to my mother's disappointment; in the first few pages I was writing about 'eligible bachelors', which she sensed, rightly, would be funny, but because I knew nothing about eligible bachelors, I stopped. Encouraged to go on, I swerved into the kind of story I was reading from my elder brother's bookshelves, full of my real love-objects of the time, horses, and with the kind of happy ending that *Mickey Mouse* turned out to like. Thus was my handwriting for the first time translated into somebody else's print.

But grammar school followed, and the Horsham High School Magazine. A succession of poems called things like 'Autumn Gold' and 'Autumn Sunset, Beachy Head' (seasonal obsession due only to the recurrent winter submission date) were printed year on year, though my English teacher suggested with a grim smile that I remove the simile, 'like menstrual blood', from my paean to reddening skies. I replaced it with 'like fading fireships', which neither of us realised was worse.

But I do remember an uneasy sense that I might be already out of date. What with schooldays and adolescent angst, I was too busy to pursue the rather modern fictional enterprise that the Budding Authoress had based on the western, so poetry became my outlet, and my masters were nineteenth-century, Tennyson, Matthew Arnold and even Swinburne. There were other, cooler girls at school, slender, arty Jane Ware, for example, dark eyes in a pale matte heart-shaped face and wiry black, well-cut hair, her wand-like waist caught in by the widest of then-fashionable wide belts; she and her friend Trisha were writing fragmented, symbolist poems of haiku brevity while I was still galumphing unstoppably through my iambic pentameters towards autumn sunsets. But Miss Robinson (strong-jawed editor of the magazine) and the other English staff approved of me. Moreover I was in the L or Latin stream, the top stream, whereas Jane had been misdirected into the G for German, from which she was only later fished up into the Latinate light (unbelievably, thinking of the

47

nervous tactfulness with which streaming is concealed today, there was also a C for Cookery class. And this was a grammar school! Stay in the kitchen, dunces.)

Swot that I was, and favoured, I chose TS Eliot's *Collected Poems* for my English Prize in 4L, and then moved reluctantly, long after beautiful Jane, into the twentieth century, haunted and enchanted by Eliot's melancholy ironies and half-lit city streets. I have it still, a hardback, blue, with 'Margaret Gee' written inside in my still coltish italic, a little stiff and self-conscious, proud, the signature of a self in the process of creation, trying to become a person, an adult writer, by taking possession of the poet. The print on the spine, 'TS Eliot', is still, forty-five years later, faintly silver, numinous.

And Jane – beautiful, gifted Jane – Jane of the haiku, swinging her violin – she died, in her twenties, of cancer.

When I compute the luck in my life, I do not forget her.

6 My animal luck (iii)

running

My first coherent memory is of brightness and movement, running on a wide flat beach at Shell Bay. I am singular, and dazzled. I am not quite three. An expanse of white light, my parents behind my brother and me, the sea a low brilliant line, far away. Something catches my eye: full-stop. I crouch to pick up a small oblong shell, even whiter than the sand, chalk-white, crisply detailed, covered with regular indentations, which to me are identical to those on my new summer shoes. I name it with absolute certainty: 'Look, I've found a Tennis White.' Everyone except my brother is very pleased with me, though I have no idea what I have done, no idea it was a metaphor. I have better things to do. I run on.

Animal luck – for ninety-five per cent of us at least – is movement. Unlike plants, animals wriggle and slide, ooze and flip, sprint like cheetahs through the Kenyan sunlight, pivot as swallows do, climb like buzzards, dive like otters. To seek out food, track down a sexual partner or parade before them, escape our enemies on a speedy wave of

Dancing on the beach

49

adrenalin. Or just move for the joy of it: dolphins spurting through blue air above the sea, foals racing across a field.

Plants, on the other hand, stay put. They can send seeds or spores to blow on the wind or hitch a lift on a passing animal, they can push suckers out through the mud and spread their genes across acres, but the parent plants must sit tight and adapt to the place where evolution has deposited them. And they do adapt, fast: the leaves of African violets grow thicker and smaller in drought, mint coarsens within weeks when evicted from kitchen to garden. Plants grow narrow and tall, or broad and bushy, to suit the light and the space they are given.

Animals, of course, can also adapt, but not as swiftly as plants. We don't need to. If things don't suit animals, we simply move on where life is easier.

Or the lucky ninety-five per cent of us do. Molluscs, for example, are less lucky. One day, in my thirties, I went to a beach in Wales with my husband and one of his friends, and we walked down a shore-side path that the friend I will call Raymond knew well. The rocks were covered with live limpets, a quiet colony of conical mid-brown shells, clamped fast to the surface. 'If you stroke them, they come off in your hands,' Raymond assured us. He stroked them. So did we. Nothing happened. 'It really works,' he insisted, still stroking. We gave up. He kept going, but was obviously getting impatient. Suddenly he kicked one, hard. It fell off on the sand. 'There,' he said. I was shocked.

I believed the limpet had feelings. I believe it had consciousness, too.

When my Aunty Eve was living through her last months, in 1993, and was intermittently confused, she began to think people were out to get me. 'Be careful,' she said, when I visited her in hospital. 'They're looking out for you. It's not safe. They're saying "Maggie Gee, Animal Rights! Maggie Gee, Animal Rights!"' Hidden beneath these fantastical warnings was the fact that she knew she had changed her will in favour of another branch of the family, and had guilty fears that I would run into them on the ward, and find out. In fact, I had guessed what she'd done, and didn't care, but poor Eve couldn't know that. "Animal Rights! Maggie Gee! Maggie Gee! Animal Rights!" The voices had hissed their way into her head.

Perhaps she'd read an early novel of mine, *The Burning Book*, published nine years before, that turned out, through no conscious conviction of mine, to be about the horrors of factory farming. I meant to write a saga of English working-class life in the twentieth century, broadly, if not literally, inspired by my parents' families, where ordinary private life and ambitions would be torn apart by two world wars and the threat of a third.

1982; the Cold War was at its height and American nuclear missiles were set to be stationed in Britain. I meant to use first-person accounts of Hiroshima as an image of a possible future. But what came out, when I sat down and wrote, was not at all what I expected. I thought about blood and bruised flesh, and found I was writing about meat. I thought about burning, pulverising; there was the meat again. I found myself writing about butchers' shops, factory farms, raw liver. This strand of imagery runs through the whole book, linking Hiroshima to the hidden violence of the high street.

And yet I had always eaten meat, and do again now. After I read what I had written, I gave it up. (Only to start again three years later, which shows how imperfectly my daylight self listens to the voice of my subconscious. I had just had a baby; I was ravenous for meat.)

I am clear about some things, though.

Although I eat animals, I am an animal. I eat animals *because* I am an animal. I am an animal, though I have a soul. And if I have a soul, all animals have souls. (Later on in this book, maybe last of all, I will try to explain – I will try to understand – what I mean by a soul.)

Perhaps the whole universe flickers with souls. Stardust skeletons, starlight souls. Perhaps American Indians are right to give thanks to the spirits of the animals they have eaten.

My father would not allow us to have pets. I longed for a dog, dreamed and pleaded, was ecstatic aged twelve when Sylvia J from next door, two years older and more sophisticated, was given a male puppy called Tufty for Christmas, a tiny, adorable, whimpering thing with tight black curls and a wet black nose. But I wasn't his mummy; Sylvia was, and she grew bored with me, and later with Tufty, and Tufty grew fatter, and soon became part of the landscape, greying, a rather dull dog who was walked subduedly down the small pebbled road by Sylvia's mother.

Though I read about dogs, horses, birds, though my Observer book told me every breed of horse and pony and I spent days discussing with my friend Janet whether we would choose an Arab or a palomino, the actual animals in my childhood were few. When we lived in Bromsgrove, between my third and sixth birthdays, our neighbours, the Wises, kept pigeons. And then Great-aunt Kit, Grandma Gee's racy, widowed younger sister, got married again, to Uncle Ted, of whom my grandmother darkly said, 'I told her, "Kit, he won't just want to hold your hand."' In any case, they were too old to have children, and instead they kept a big red setter called Tess, a beautiful, rangy dog with sad eyes and a silken coat. Uncle Ted's garden led down to the river. The great excitement became fishing with a line (though fish, we were told, had to be put back, and my father said even that was cruel) with Tess in ecstatic, leaping attendance, bounding all over the river bank.

Then there was the dead sheep we found on a walk. It was spring, we were wrapped up warm, but the sheep, which lay sprawled on its side by the path, had a buzzing retinue of flies above it. As usual we children had run on ahead. 'Mum, Dad, look, it's a sheep!' I was off the path, as excited as Tess. Only a few broken strands of barbed wire lay between me and my love object. 'Get back!' my dad commanded. 'Get right away from there, Margaret!' 'But I wanter see!' I whined, thwarted. 'It's DEAD, Daddy! I wanter see it!' Instead we children were hurried away. I suppose they were frightened of whatever killed the sheep, rabies, scrapie, foot and mouth, and besides, my father had his pathological horror of death. But because we were forbidden to look at it, the image of the dead thing burned into my mind.

Animals in the human world often seemed sad. We did get a hamster; naturally, it died. Still living at Bromsgrove, so I must have been around five, my parents took me to the circus for a treat. I only remember the menagerie, which we went to afterwards, in a big, dark tent. Hopeless beasts lay about in the shadows. The smell of urine was fierce and rank. My father and mother were indignant, so I copied them. 'Maggie Gee, Animal Rights.'

Yet my father, who tended to stock positions which he cleaved to with moralising passion, disapproved of emotional views of animals. 'Some people like animals more than humans. Some people like animals more than children!' He was outraged at this lack of humanity. Socialists often feel like this. His position seemed to me unquestionable, and as children do, I adopted it myself. I was very slow to find a way of thinking not wholly centred in my own species. But perhaps I wasn't as slow as all that, because many people cannot bear to sustain the loss of pride involved in knowing we are 'just animals'.

When did I start to see it was true? I think I was probably around forty. My body, which I loved, had failed me by beginning on a series of miscarriages. I saw my will and my hope, both unlimited, were tethered to my mortal, animal body. 'Today's women want it all,' crowed the magazines of the '80s and '90s, though the claim had already begun to sound hollow, 'you can have it all, you can have it now.' This siren song was a lie, of course. Because only a very few, very lucky, women have more than one child after forty.

Biology is unmoved by our rights, unaffected by women's changing hopes and dreams. My eggs had been ageing like any chimpanzee's while I followed my glad little human trajectory of ambition, and then came the belated realisation that I longed for something outside myself. We wanted a baby. No, we wanted two babies. But the Fates came in and stared at me, hard, three frightening old women I might one day become, wielding their terrible steel scissors and thread, as the surgeons did who performed the D and Cs that tidied me up each time things went wrong. The Fates were in the gaze of the implacable nurse who came and bent over the bed where I cried silently in hospital after the operation. 'This is nothing,' she said, her eyes sharp with dislike. 'Miscarriage is common. Get over it.'

You can't have everything, the Parcae hissed, bearing down on me with furious eyes. I had flouted them, and I would be punished. *You never understood. You left it too late. You aren't special, you're an animal.*

I have always been slow to understand the big things. Quick at small things, with a slick grasp of logic, but slow at seeing the things that matter. So I didn't start to see I had a body at the stage when it might have been expected. At puberty, say. Or when I became sexual.

In any case the latter thing was somewhat delayed by my going to a traditional girls' grammar school, where you did not have to think about boys – indeed I was puzzled by the minority of girls who queued up to titivate in the cloakroom mirror: what were they so passionate about? I simply did not, at that age, get it, for my body was disconnected from my mind. Which from infants' school had nurtured bedtime fantasies of being kidnapped by bold boys on horseback, pressed against a wall and then what?

Nothing. I had no idea. The dream petered out and I went to sleep.

Not even when I had my first shy experience, aged sixteen, while acting in a play, Jonson's *The Alchemist*. I wore a beautiful pale gold satin dress sewn with paste jewels, which showed my bust, and was told (thank God. I was too naïve to think of it myself) not to wear my winged Edna Everage glasses. Playing against me was eighteen-year-old Frank Lammas, a sturdy farm boy with a soft Sussex burr, dark eyes, glossy thick hair like a blackbird's wing, and a motorbike. A motorbike! I would never have dared aspire to Frank Lammas, but somehow (perhaps it was the removal of my glasses) Frank Lammas saw something sensual in the woman I played. Frank began stroking and caressing my hands, tender, intimate, sweetest of touches, and his kisses became, not stage kisses, but real. Nothing so good had ever happened to me. When we weren't acting, only little looks and smiles showed that the impossible was true: beautiful Frank Lammas fancied me. Since he was in the sixth form at my father's school, nothing more daring was ever going to happen, and my father was already becoming suspicious. After the final performance, Frank Lammas offered me a lift on his motorbike, at twenty miles per hour, just around the school car park, and then this happy chapter of my life was over. But thank you, dear Frank, for seeing the woman in me. Your sunlight touched me. I could grow towards it.

I have always loved, and enjoyed, my body, though I didn't listen to what it told me. I liked being able to run and climb. I approved of my body; it did what it should. I had to be a tomboy, to be like my brothers, but I also remember distinctly, aged thirteen, looking in the mirror and seeing new breasts above my ribcage. Yes, I thought smugly, just as I expected, they are coming out perfectly, as they would (later, of course, I would learn, through pain, that the body I loved was imperfect, frangible). I enjoyed, above all, the sensation of speed, for I had always been a good runner, which translated, with age, into being a sprinter, a skill which stood me in good stead at school. The very children who tormented me gave me a half-admiring nickname: 'MG Fast Car', said as all one word, because I could get away from them, and I often had to, on the way home, as they pursued me, half-serious, down the church path. I preferred it so much to 'Gee-gee', or the worst name of all, 'Dobbin's daughter', which cut me to the quick because it meant my father, Mr Gee the secondary school headmaster, was secretly called 'Dobbin' by my classmates' elder brothers. 'MG-Fast-Car' was expensive, racy.

Being able to run got me grudging respect, whereas doing well at lessons caused only hatred, in that village school in Billingshurst where out of forty-three children in Mr Upton's class, only 'me and Ivor Laker' passed the eleven plus and got into grammar school. But everyone had bodies. Everyone did sport.

Both my parents had been athletic, my father a footballer and middle distance runner, my mother a sprinter, hurdler, hockey-player, with the result that they became perhaps too involved in my success as a teenage athlete. But races can only have one winner. Mostly I did win my races at school, and in my fourth year at grammar school, just before I gave up, amassed the most points on Sports Day, as both of them had in the days when this honour was called victor, or victrix, ludorum. I competed as a junior for my county: won some small medals, their silver now grey, with the blue Sussex shield blazoned with small yellow birds. Trained, for a while, with Brighton Ladies Athletic club, in shocking pink tops and streamlined black satin shorts, and won, on one glorious day in London, the hundred metres at a big inter-club meet. (I came back and told Grandpa Gee, the former sprinter, now buckled by a stroke, strapped into black, built-up, surgical boots, and living with us as he struggled back to fitness, only to suffer another stroke. He laughed with joy. Margaret had trounced the Londoners! 'Well done girl! That showed them.' That day I was his granddaughter as never before.)

But the changing-rooms, the jockery, began to repel me, and in retrospect, I never could have been top flight. I wasn't quite tall or long-limbed enough. Besides, something important was being forgotten, with all the adrenalin and nervousness, the warming up, the weight-training, and my parents asking eagerly if I had won.

The joy of it. That was what had gone. The thing I had felt on the beach as a toddler, when my stubby little feet and my chubby child legs sped up until they passed the vital line between walking and running, when both feet are off the ground at once. That precious thing, pure movement. Gravity defeated, the lift into flight. The thing that comes to anyone running full-tilt, without pain or pressure, the real joy of the sprint, the all-subsuming sense that you and your body are one, and the unity is weightless, sheer speed, pure flow. You are not lifting or moving anything; nothing is moving or lifting you. You are the movement. You are in flight. Pure animal alchemised into spirit.

One other time I felt the same joy, something atavistic that predates modern humans, their vegetable state briefly interrupted by panting, sweating sessions down the gym. Now activity is seen as a self-limiting episode, whereas, once, surely, life was motion.

When John and I were teenagers, and my little brother was ten years younger, our parents took us on camping trips so we could afford to go abroad. We didn't have a car, which might have stymied some people, but we loaded our camping gear into prams and push-chairs, which somehow or other we heaved on to trains (consider the terror at European stations, as the huge foreign expresses roared in beside the platform and we had to get two prams and a pushchair on board, from the hoods of which the round bottoms of duffel-bags looked out, the small brass studs like a pair of piggy eyes, the body of the prams full of tents, billy-cans, cooking-stoves, wind-breaks, sleeping-bags, provisions. Imagine my father, marshalling his troops! Three prams, his three children, a friend each for John and me, his wife, his precious camera-bag, his briefcase, rucksacks for my father and the two elder boys. Three vehicles, five children, a pile of bags and baggages. Looking back on it all, I salute you, Dad. I forgive the bawlings-out as we panicked on to trains.)

One fine July day we had gone for a day-trip up high in the Swiss mountains on a crawling funicular train, with slatted wooden seats. Despite my fear, it did not hesitate, groan, and plummet with terrible speed back down the mountain. When we got to the top, Dad set off boldly in the opposite direction from all the other passengers. This stratagem was not always successful, but this time it brought us to a paradisal place, ringed by snow-topped peaks but curiously temperate, a lightly-wooded, green-turfed valley with a river and a grassy path meandering beside it, little patches of silver river-sand and stones.

My friend Janet and I were perhaps thirteen. We were just beginning to be adolescents, but as childhood friends, we could be children together, which is one definition of happiness. Sometimes Nick and I are children together. Janet was one of the non-bullyers at junior school, one of the people who have shown me that hope is worthwhile, for some people's hearts are immune to peer pressure, some children have been treated with enough kindness to be kind to others when they're very young. Janet had decided to be my friend, and she even withstood my astonished lack of trust: 'Are you REALLY my friend? Promise?' How many times did I interrogate her? 'I am your friend. Why do you keep asking?' And my answer, from the voice of pure misery in my chest – 'Because no one likes me, since my parents left Bromsgrove and they put me up a class, no one's ever liked me' – was stilled in the end. Janet liked me. And so did Anne Simmers. And so did Linda Tucker. Janet also loved running, as I did.

My parents let the children off the leash, that day, for a few hours. Freedom! We were walking fast, then we started to run. Janet and I were running, easily. We ran by the mountain river in the clear, snow-cooled early afternoon sunlight, passing young silver birches and slender conifers, down the easy path through tasselled grasses, with the river on the left and my family still way behind us. And something happened; we were not going to stop, we were on our second wind, and our third, no longer counting, we had turned into the horses we used to dream of, we were animals, we could run for ever, had slipped back in history, and before history, we were loping, now, across the sun-bright savannah. We had no limit. We became movement. We ran for hours beside the river, through the sunlit country, past rocks and trees.

Of course I wore a watch, and the hours slipped away, and by the time we got back, my father was cross because my brother and his friend were late; but the memory has stayed with me, unchanging, complete, an image of cloudless physical life.

As we age, such moments come less often. At its worst, the body becomes something to forget or to carry, something best ignored, something to transcend, a net of competing pain-signals.

But my body for the most part is still my friend. Bodies *must* be our friends, or they will turn against us. When I neglect my body, it reminds me, sharply. When I overwork: when I forget to walk.

I see cyber-life, the virtual, as the enemy. It keeps this generation of young in dark rooms, leaching strength from their arms and suppleness from their shoulders, poking their heads forwards like unshelled tortoises. It sucks out their souls through their eye-sockets. Poor young people, kept from the light.

Here at St Cuthman's, Neville said, 'God did not make you for the dark of death, but to live.'

To live. In our bodies, in the light, may we live.

In Vladimir Nabokov's great novel *Ada,* the hero, Van Veen, ages from a child to an old man, but Nabokov teasingly tells us that in his eighties Van still dances on his hands – 'I can do anything, I can tango and tap-dance on my fantastic hands' – delaying and delaying the final sigh of information that this is 'only in a recurrent dream'.

True, the mind can hold what the body has given. I dream of running, fast and free, an easy circuit through sand and silver birches, with the amazed (but delusory) realisation that I am still running as fast as ever.

But a dream goes cold on waking. I run, for real, on London roads, not far, but enjoying it, listening to my feet, counting magpies and urban blossom, ignoring aches and car-fumes. I hope to go on running till I die. I hope to go on having sex till I die. Not only in dreams, but in the warmth of the flesh. I'm thinking about orgasm, now. What a beautiful expression 'coming' is. I'm coming, moving, here in the moment, here in the body, running wild.

7 My parents change class

not in the way they expected

Here is one of my questions: in a single lifetime, do you ever, truly, change class?

In one sense, that of appearances, class changes in a flash, leaping slick as a fish over the weir in a mere two decades. Send a child to public school and Oxbridge, or Harvard, or the Sorbonne, and even if the grandparents' families have been sons and daughters of the soil for thirty generations, no one will be any the wiser. Will they?

No one except the child. Each child instinctively knows where they come from, what their earliest memories are, which smells, which comforts, what their uncles and aunts were like, how they speak, how they eat. When they hear those voices again, wherever they are, however many years later, they will prick up their ears; hail, friend. (Though some of course are ashamed.)

So what class am I? I'm a novelist – middle-class profession – and went to Oxford – middle-class education – and am married to a man who went to public school and Oxford, and knows the names of his family back to the seventeenth century – middle-class man. I like expensive scent, Issey Miyake or Chanel No 5 or 19, or Jo Malone, and good wine; I have flown to Australia, over the curve of the earth where suddenly St Petersburg glittered below on the night like a handspread of stars, and worked in Berlin and Vienna, and trodden the stones of the Roman road to Carthage, at Leptis Magna, Libya. I saw lions in the pink early morning in Uganda; I have wandered through the Prado, and been moved to tears by the tender arches and vaults of a Gaudí building in Barcelona. Middle-class pleasures, middle-class tears; middle-class, I must be. Yet at the deepest level, am I?

Not if the deepest level is the oldest, the thing-that-you-know-before-knowing-you-are-thinking, no, I am not just that.

Because I was born into those two families, the Gees and the Churches, both working-class through and through: and a grain of their toughness, an inherited sense of being an outsider looking slightly askance at what the privileged get up to, remains at the core of my adult self. True, my parents, Vic and Aileen, let their brains take them as far as they could from Bucks and outside plumbing and the narrowness of terraces.

Was it easy to move away? It must have been exciting, striking out on their own, going southwards, sunwards to Hazlemere and then Poole, where they knew nobody, to raise their young family. For my mother at first it was a liberation; in the final year of the war she had had to care for a baby, my brother John, living with the family of her absent husband in Wolverton, afraid that the baby's crying would wake up her 'cut above' in-laws, the Gees. Once Vic was home from India, Aileen became entangled in the web of Gee-family over-sensitivity. She told me that every day she was afraid Dad might find his prone-to-tears mother crying, in which case he would come and find her and ask, 'What have you been doing to upset Ma?' The idea of their own place in the south, away from all this, was intoxicating.

I mustn't think going so far was simple for them. Most Gees and Churches stayed put, keeping the habits and social links they were born with. It was easier for my parents to move than to arrive. There's a grain of something concretely real in that unpleasantly snobbish term 'arriviste'. Because arriving in a new class isn't something you do and then forget; it can be a never-ending, restless state. You leave

John, Mum, Dad and me, five years before younger brother James was born

once, but always continue to look for a welcome, and follow clues how to behave.

New houses! That was what they wanted, new beginnings. 'New build'. The thing that my generation avoids unless they can afford something edgy and architect-built. But Vic and Aileen both wanted to escape the dark and the fustiness. They had come through the war! Young marrieds on the cusp between their twenties and thirties. Both fiercely clever in different ways and recognising that quality in each other, they were eager for the future, but the first few houses they lived in – Hazlemere, Poole, Barnt Green, Bromsgrove, Watersfield, because my father was ambitious for promotions in teaching and they kept on the move – were all compromise, pre-war housing, one Edwardian, one 1940s, and so on.

How they loved the idea of their first all-new home. The Croft, Oaklands, Billingshurst, Sussex, where they moved in 1956, when

I was seven, was a three-bed cross between a house and a bungalow, with two downstairs bedrooms for the children. My parents' bedroom and loo, side by side with my father's darkroom for photography, were perched on their own, upstairs. Built new for them! They fell in love (via the pencil drawings, which they proudly showed their children) with the big semi-circular bay window at the front, which took up half the width of the house. Both had their own sense of beauty, and a wish to be different, though my father's was constrained by a streak of fearful conservatism he denied; between them they chose, to curtain that giant bay, a repeated small 1960s line-drawing of a man driving a donkey-cart, back view, which promised them holidays, relaxation, the country, all things which proved not so easy to find; but they bought it in three different pastel colours, giving a daring rainbow effect when the curtains were closed. In that window, in the blaze of sun, stood also my father's 'Stereomaster', a radio-cum-record-player of monumental dimensions, with late 1950s splayed legs and a cabinet of pale wood (which my mother secretly disliked: 'It's like a coffin,' she whispered to me, once its novelty wore off. No wonder she resented it when no one but Dad was allowed to touch it; he was extending his musical tastes, and liked to have female opera-singers, out of Radio 3, at breakfast; 'that bloomin' screaming', Mum called it.)

But on the drawing-board this house, for us all, was to be perfect, the final stage in our ascension from Bucks, via Poole (and a small retreat, *reculer pour mieux sauter*, to the midlands) to Sussex. My own part of the excitement was choosing paint for my bedroom. Remember the rarity of luxury and colour in that austere post-war world of the fifties, the scarcity of ornament and print. So the paint manufacturer's cards with their tiny neat pools of gloss or matte colour, dozens of shades all subtly different, the smell of the cardboard and the feel to my fingertips of the cool slippery gloss, were artefacts of rare beauty. Each small bright rectangle of paint had a number which led you to a correspondingly wonderful name:

Jasmine Yellow, Duck-egg Blue, Apricot Pink. I changed my mind over and over again.

Yet the room, when finally unveiled, was a bad disappointment. I was sure that my parents had muddled up my choices. One wall was a murky blue-green, one a fleshy, overbearing pinky-orange, two were yellow, and clashed with the pink. And there were acid yellow curtains with a pattern of rickshaw-pulling coolies with pigtails; I definitely hadn't chosen *those*. I raged and complained.

My poor parents. They had wanted me to be pleased, and let me choose. Instead I made everyone unhappy. I insisted, and cried, and screamed, that I had never chosen these horrors. I wanted to be *myself*. My family was totally unsatisfactory.

Looking back, what threw me was the difference between real paint and the ideal poetry of names.

We lived in the Croft for two decades, until the mid-seventies, for my father had got his headship ('I was one of the youngest heads in the country'), and stayed until retirement, his youth worn away, jaw jutting forward with the strain of the job to which he walked off every morning, a three-minute walk in his long grey-beige gaberdine mack to the big modern school at the bottom of our garden which he steered from a secondary modern to one of the first comprehensives. My brother John and I grew up and became adolescents, though we weren't modern teenagers at all. John, tall and skinny with very long arms, a vulnerable Adam's apple, full sensual lips and a brilliant mathematical brain, came effortlessly top of all subjects at his excellent grammar school, Colyers, and was a demon fast bowler in the Billingshurst cricket team, 'over-bowled' by the captain, as Dad said, despairingly, thinking of future arthritis as John pounded away summer Saturdays notching up wickets. John was a Manchester United fan like my father, and went out with the girl next door. What better son could be imagined? My father loved him to a painful degree, yet he fought with him; too much testosterone under one roof. I too was a good teenager in many ways, a bad one in others. Like John, I was both a swot and a sports fiend; I was sexually innocent, neither drank nor took drugs (I was saving things up for later, getting up a head of pressure so the eventual explosion would be worthwhile). Yes, I tormented my kind mother with cruel remarks, refused to eat with my family, read half the night, hated my father, started to be weird about food. But in public terms, both John and I were successes. In private we raged and stormed and, in the end, partially curbed ourselves; one by one, as raw seventeen-year-olds, before things could get too bad, we went away. Another brother was born, the baby of the family, Jamey or James, nearly ten years younger than me, a blond-curled, blue-eyed boy of great beauty and perfect eyesight, whereas John and I were both wiry bespectacled children with knobbly joints and big ears, then awkward adolescents who couldn't wait to be twenty. In time James became a teenager, actually a teenager, unlike his two elder siblings, dancing to T-Rex, being a proto-communist, bringing girlfriends home. And as all these things happened Vic and Aileen aged from their thirties into their fifties, and certain things became set, and others, in the hothouse of our adolescence, burst and broke, and some of the hopes of the big sunny bay were disappointed, and others, for the next generation's success, were exceeded.

From the springboard of the local grammar schools, those engines of class mobility which the current Labour government considers undemocratic, both my elder brother John and I won Major Oxford Scholarships, John's in Physics and mine in English, while my political younger brother James (now Jim, but still unnaturally handsome) went to the best place for politics, LSE. Our parents were so proud, too proud for good sense.

Easy to understand why, since Vic and Aileen were easily as clever as their children, but were doomed by their class, and in my mother's case, gender, not to have the education they deserved. (My mother, like her sister Eve, couldn't continue her education after her 'Highers', because what little money the parents had was earmarked for the boys' apprenticeships, even though the girls were brighter than the boys; only Eve and Aileen 'passed the scholarship' at eleven to the grammar school. 'We thought nothing of it,' said my mother, of the way the money went to her brothers. 'It was just the way things were.') My father had done an external, thus affordable, degree in geography, art, religious knowledge and PE at St Luke's College, Exeter, which he did not rate highly. On the wall of our dining-room now is a black-and-white watercolour he did of the room where he stayed. 'CORNER OF ROOM: 4-WASH TONAL EXERCISE, 1935,' the title written in his meticulously pencilled capital letters, underlined with obvious use of a ruler. It is a beautiful thing, because Vic had a real gift for drawing, as did his brother Lloyd who, apprenticed in the Railway Works, eventually rose to become the designer of the Queen's Train. But the room in my father's vision is claustrophobic, the bed ultra-narrow, the corner cluttered with bleak furniture, the window barred though the sunlight comes in a flood through one side of the curtain, the shadow in the corner very dark.

No wonder they channelled their own unfulfilled ambitions through us. What they had deserved, we would get. John and I always had to be not just the brightest but the youngest, both going to Oxford as painfully raw seventeen-year-olds, which was a tragic mistake, since if children are pushed on ahead of their peer group they grow lopsided, like a plant with only one side turned to the light. My childhood emotions and social skills never had a chance to catch up with my brains.

Many of my mistakes as an adult I could put down to this accelerated childhood, which cut me off from the peer group that sensible parents know is the only place, more than universities or prizes, where acceptance matters. To be liked, known, at ease, with good friends; it's another part of happiness, *pace* Proust (and who wants to spend their life on their own, like him, in a cork-lined room, writing in bed? Occasionally, when the phone or email stops me writing, I envy him, but not very often.)

Pushed up into a class of eleven-year-olds at school when I was only nine, and in any case, coming from another part of England as I did, always a foreigner to my new giant Billingshurst classmates, the sturdy children of Sussex farmers and cleaners and builders; weedy and small, weighing only four stone when I arrived at the school in my skew-whiff pink National Health glasses, and sickeningly praised by the teachers, my fate was sealed.

'Your mum and dad do your homework.' 'They don't.' 'They do.' 'You stole your story from a book.' 'I didn't.' 'You did.' 'Your family is posh' – but I knew they were not. There were arm-twistings and slaps in the cloakroom from the glamorous Lamb twins, Joyce and Jean, and pushing and shoving and Chinese burns in the bike-sheds from the butcher's fat carrot-top son Peter Sawyer and his sinister bright-blue-blazered, wedge-headed friend, who surely cannot have been, as I remember him, German, and called Kurt or Karl? (Of course it is possible. Looking back, the bullies are often the misfits, and we were still close to the war.)

But the Lambs – ah, the Lambs – they were different. Joyce – straight blonde hair and pretty – and Jean – dark curls, freckly animal face, a good runner but more of a bully than her sister – were queens of popularity, practically film stars, polished and posh, to me, as fresh paint, and though they hated and oppressed me, I wanted nothing on earth so much as myself to possess their grey pleated skirts, tight yellow polo neck jumpers, and most of all, so much that I almost desire them still, cherry-red corduroy trousers: banned by the headmaster, for fear of establishing a trend, within a week.

Mum did her best. Billingshurst just had a wool shop, so she had only the limited resources of Horsham's premier department store, musty Chart and Lawrence, at her disposal, to assuage my passionate pleas for clothes like Joyce's and Jean's. Perhaps I thought they would make me look like a big girl instead of the skinny little weirdo I was.

But no, there was nothing rational about my longing, it was just love. The Lambs were like girls in books, a perfect pair, because each, as in stories, had a ready-made best friend; they had stepped straight from the front page of *Girl*, dark Wendy and shining blonde Jinx, with their narrow red legs or knife-edge grey pleats, their sunshine yellow tops and victorious smiles. I instructed my mother (as I thought) in the exact items to be bought; I had had no new clothes since for ever; now I could only wait.

Poor Mum. She must have gone on the train to Horsham and braved the old dragons of Chart and Lawrence. But in those days shop assistants saw my mother coming; despite her carefully narrowed vowels, for which a Gee uncle once mimicked her on a Wolverton bus. (An insult my loving mother never forgot. Oh class! How it makes us fear each other's judgements. 'Trying to be posh.' 'Not posh enough.') She came back, indeed, with a pleated skirt, and most daringly, trousers. She was excited, but also afraid. She had taken a risk; my father never let her wear trousers, for in my sharply gendered family, trousers were for boys (which, in the great economy of action-reaction, must be why I now nearly always wear them).

Trousers and a skirt! Two new garments at once, and not on her birthday, for little Marg! Ungrateful churl that I was, I took one look, and pretended to like them, but within ten minutes, collapsed into sulks. The skirt was slightly hairy wool plaid, and brown. It was ordinary. No one would notice it, or admire it, or want to be my friend. The trousers, or what Mum called 'trews', were red, as she pleadingly pointed out, but they were *dull* red, orangey ('I *hate* that colour, it's horrible'), not corduroy, and made even darker by a pattern of small black dog-tooth check. And in any case by the next Monday, when I might have worn them, trousers were banned.

But not by my father, not for me. This was the fascinating, terrible thing about my father; though, as long as he could, until I was fourteen or fifteen, he banned anything potentially sexual in my life, such as layered haircuts, mascara, lipstick, high heels; though until

I was ten I was never allowed to walk even as far as the station (400 yards) on my own, he eventually encouraged me to do all manner of things – work, travel, be independent, try to be famous – that his wife was forbidden. Why? I think now that because I was half him, and *he* could do anything, I could do anything too. I have heard of other fathers who do exactly the same – urge the daughters onward, keep the mother close at home.

The injustice was obvious to both of us, but Mum was generous, and rejoiced in my relative freedom. She said wistfully, sometimes, after all her three children had finished their qualifications, 'I'm the only person in the family without a degree.' Dad would be brusque and dishonest: 'You're cleverer than all of us, you know you are Aileen. You don't need a qualification to prove it.' Of course, she did need it. I heard that exchange too often.

Never tell someone else what they do or don't need.

In the end, Mum got what she needed, by leaving, after all the three kids had gone out into the world, after Vic had retired and they had left the Billingshurst community where separation would have meant disgrace in the married middle class they had moved to.

It didn't last. In my memory it was only weeks. My father was astonished, and despairing, because he adored, and depended on, Aileen. Because she was afraid, she left him without warning. Took the car, and fled to me, who by then was doing a PhD in Wolverhampton. I had to pretend, in answer to my father's desperate phone calls, to know nothing. As I write this I still feel frightened, because Aunty Eve, who knew Vic didn't like her, told us, in case we softened, 'We think he's got a car and he's coming to find you.' And so my mother and I set off on a panicky zigzag trip round unpleasant cheap hotels in Northamptonshire and Leicestershire. The logic behind this was never spelled out, though Mum's niece Jeanette, her elder sister's daughter, with whom she had lost touch, was fabled to keep a pub called 'The Red Cow' in Kirby Muxloe near

Leicester, and in my researches since I have discovered that one side of Mum's family, the Meakinses, had frequented Northamptonshire for generations. So maybe she was trying to go home, to shelter in the folds of a lost name. In any case, it didn't work; we rushed around like moths trying to escape from a light that searched us out and drew us back. The terror of it was, '*He's coming after you.*'

Traumatic. I was twenty-seven, but the idea of my parents splitting up was unthinkable, much though I wanted my mother to be free of fear, and have the life she wanted. She had talked about leaving for years, but only to me, and of course, loving her, I could not dissuade her. I wanted her to be happy because the pity I felt for her unhappiness was unbearable for me.

But how would they cope on their own? Could there be a Mummy without a Daddy, a Daddy without a Mummy? Inside, at this critical moment, I was still six years old. I suspect that somewhere in every child whose parents split up is this helpless terror; the foundations of the world are shaken. The rigid shell that contained all the anger and fear in that marriage had broken, and now it was everywhere, glistening and quivering, terrible, revealed in the open. Every night Mum slept with a knife under her pillow, every day we drove somewhere with me sitting beside her, sedating myself by drinking British sherry from the bottle.

But the truth was very different from Eve's report. My father was not angry, he was overwhelmed with grief. He had not tried to get a car to replace the one Mum had taken, and in any case had no idea where to find her, though later (perhaps in order to protect his love for me) he always pretended to think she'd spent the time away from him, not with me, as was the case, but with Eve and Albert, who of course he disliked already. When Aileen discovered that he only wanted her back, her resolve crumbled, and she became tearful. Her whole demeanour changed; now she felt she was doing wrong.

Within weeks she was negotiating to go back, or rather, in agony, I was. We all three met at another hotel, gloomy and English; a stiff meal at a small round table. There were obvious conditions, such as no more frightening behaviour and money of her own in a separate account; and there were touching ones, such as 'us to have friends', 'us to have interests'. He agreed to everything, and improvising, I threw in one Mum had not had time to think of: 'She wants to do a degree. She's determined.' 'Your mother doesn't need a degree.' 'Well she *wants* one, Dad.' This time he conceded.

1977. And now their lives changed and expanded. Though my father had left his job two years earlier, this was the point when they started to live like the retired professional people with a good pension that they actually were. My mother registered to do a Humanities degree at the Open University. They marched round and knocked on the door of another couple their age, the Bishops, who also lived on Barratt Road: 'We want to be friends.' According to my mother, my father actually said those very words, unconsciously ticking off one of her conditions. Silver-haired John Bishop and his wife were just right, as friends; he was, I think, a retired tax officer, something not too different from a retired head teacher, and like Dad, he painted. They had the same size house, the same kind of car (Mum and Dad had by now pulled back from their belligerent, armour-plated Landrover into a pearly-green Golf, or rather a succession of Golfs, bought new, by my father's rigid theory, changed every year), the same kind of mildly Germanic walking shoes and not-quite-country-coloured quilted rain-jackets. The same voices, within the same unthreatening range of accents, not posher than us, just right. And John Bishop painted and drew just well enough to be a worthy friend for Vic, but not too well, so as make him jealous.

Now they had friends. For the first time, they entertained.

(And here I must make a digression in order to explain what this meant. For throughout my childhood, the only people who came to the house in Billingshurst when my father was home were the following:-

Family. Rarely, because they nearly all lived north of us, and besides, there were eggshells they had to step lightly across. But the extended Gee family was, like my father, loyal.

Once, as a duty, the newly arrived head of Billingshurst Junior School, Mr Shaw, and his lean and racy wife Jackie ('She's like a yappy little dog,' said my Mum, unused to female competition, and 'He's vain,' said my Dad, having noticed, correctly, how my primary head teacher used his blue flashing eyes and surprised upright gingerish brows to command attention).

The woodwork teacher from my father's school, Dougie Henderson, and his beautiful, soft-fleshed wife Margaret, who by their sheer physical dark-eyed charm and aura of perpetual laughter – were they Jewish or Italian, somewhere? More likely Scots, for Dad always had a soft spot for Scots – won my father over, made him feel safe (though both Mum and I were in love with the dark-jawed, dark-eyed, incredibly relaxed and soigné, slightly chubby Dougie Henderson; could men really be warm and tender and funny?)

Lastly, once a year, 'the Louis', Roger and Christiane Louis, always called 'Monsieur and Madame Louis' by us, the French teachers who came to Sussex with the French school with whom my father's school did foreign exchanges. My mother put roses from the garden in the bedroom, but Monsieur Louis removed them with a charming apology, saying, 'My wife says they are too smelly,' which made my mother, in secret, laugh almost as much as the time Madame Louis, conversing at tea, referred to Margot Fonteyn: 'she ees a very great Ballot-woman. I theenk,' which might have been all right had my eyes not met my mother's, whereupon she summoned me from the room 'to help in the kitchen', where we both collapsed, weeping and knocking our heads on the rose-pink Formica worktop in an attempt to muffle our laughter.

Oh, and the vicar, the Reverend Evan-Hopkins, once called for tea. The Rev Ev, as we called him, lacked the common touch. When told about the camping holiday we planned in Switzerland, the poor man said, in the fluting tones he could not help, 'Everything on your backs, I think you're marvellous.' The Rev Ev was unfeasibly tall and weedy, his admiration for our peasant frames probably sincere, but it stung my father, after the vicar was gone, to cynical laughter. Thenceforth 'Everything on your backs' was Dad's catchphrase for the vicar.

I make that seven people in total. Some of those once, twice at most. Many of the events marked by tension, social anxiety, and afterwards the 'bloomin' inquest' in which my mother thought my father specialised. No wonder I began adult life as a social cripple, exhausted by gatherings of more than five people, terrified of parties, where, if I actually got through the door, I gabbled nonsense. Only in my last decade have I realised that I enjoy entertaining. Thus I follow the parental pattern, only slightly younger than Mum and Dad were when they first blossomed.

Now I see that this, too, was all about class. Having left the close communities of Bucks where everyone was roughly the same, where no one could feel out of place because every street and house was alike, my parents were lost. You can leave the working-class, through sheer energy and drive, but never quite arrive anywhere else. *Arrivistes*! We lived in limbo, 'new build'.)

Mum and Dad took three decades to learn the basics of middle-class social life. Firstly, a drinks cupboard, a post-separation innovation which they stocked lavishly with middle-class sweetish drinks with glamorous names like Dubonnet, Cinzano Bianco, Martini, but hardly used (we children repaired to it regularly, to cushion our fear of what had briefly been out in the open and now, after a brief reordering, was being shoved back out of sight again). Secondly, friends. Two was a milestone, but the world opened up when they started adult education classes in Norwich, at Wensum Lodge. Life regained structure and meaning. It was a forty-five-minute drive from Holt to Norwich, and a forty-five-minute drive back, but they went three times a week. More surprisingly, they actually went to different classes – my mother to Spanish and Creative Writing, my father to Drawing and Painting. (This was almost miraculous; they had been welded at the hip for decades, with my mother unable to shop, or visit the doctor, or have coffee with her daughter, or go up to London, on her own. This was the new regime, and surely a relief for Vic as well as Aileen. If you never leave your wife alone, can she ever freely come back?)

At Wensum Lodge, Vic did not have to control things. The teacher, at last, could relax into being taught. Vic idolised his teachers, one in particular, Peter Jamieson, who did fine-grained black-and-white woodcuts, one of which hangs in our dining-room now, an arch of profusely detailed oak-leaves framing a sheltered garden with cow parsley in bloom, in the middle ground a house whose roof protects the onlooker from the sun's aureole, blazing behind the chimney. How happy Dad was to buy it: 'Exhibited in RA Show 1972'. *Fear no more the heat o' the sun.* And the foibles of their classmates, mostly retired, of course, were an interest. My father was still prone to prickliness, especially with males – this one was 'a show-off', that one 'a big mouth' or 'too big for his boots' – but many of them he grew fond of; retirement meant he no longer had to stay top of the heap. Time for a rest.

You could say, if you wanted to be reductive, that the final and furthest point of their escape from the old dark class was a new brick bungalow in Barrett Road so small they could never, once they had shut the back door with its big glass panel, get away from each other; thin walls, matchstick-flat doors, too hot and, as Dad's eyes became worse, too brilliantly lit, almost a stage-set, with enormous 150-watt bulbs and additional fluorescent strips, like futuristic light-swords, bearing down on the small kitchen-diner where they ate; with a featureless grass-and-geranium garden, a rolled-door garage and a tiny turquoise bathroom. Sometimes going home felt grim.

But I know that from their point of view, the years brought something kinder. Age is a class and a place of its own, with its dress code of comfortable, washable warm clothes that most people wear, its permission, for my father, to wear a track suit top sometimes (they were new and European to him, not a sign of the underclass) instead of a head teacher's jacket and tie; its unifying drill of small movements through which the old signal to each other, its cap-badge of grey or white hair. Its own accents, finally nothing to do with the class they were born to, slight breathlessness, an increasing softness or harshness.

Its own comforts. With a lifetime of duties eased away, time for those: couples walking the narrow pavements in the afternoon, matching heads, bent forwards, gilded by winter sun; 'days out', trips to the sea to watch birds and boats. Educating themselves, their souls expanding; instead of being educators, putting out year after year until, like bulbs, they were exhausted. Glasses of warm Ribena, my father's favourite, brought to him almost hourly by my mother, all day long.

Not just comforts, but luxuries (from the point of view of the class my parents were born to) and new pleasures. For my mother, though my father was ashamed of her for being frank and saying so, money. The mortgage paid off, the pension arriving every month so they actually told us they felt, if not rich, 'quite well-off'. My mother's joy in knowing she would never be poor while my father was alive (and her paradoxical unwillingness to accept that she *would* be poor, barring a miracle – or as it turned out, cancer – once he was dead.) The money was not just the thick silken feel of the notes she took, every time with wonder and gratitude, from the hole in the wall, but the freedom to spend. How she enjoyed her food shopping trips to Holt on her spanking red bike with the basket on the front (Vic still, even after the beginning of the New Life, didn't like her to take the car on her own, perhaps because it brought back memories of her driving away and not coming back.) What she carried proudly home was often what she called 'a bit of lux, eh Marg?' – the antithesis of the plain food of the 1940s and '50s, a living denial of the meagreness of rations in the house on London Road when she was a child. Anything with spices or something unlikely super-added would appeal to her: 'Come on, let's try it!' She wanted superfluity for its own sake, partly to show that she could and partly because, in the seventies and eighties, it was suddenly on offer. Decades of plenty! Stuffed olives, sugared ham, pickled walnuts, ready-made sauces in bottles that made extravagant promises. 'Rich' things: Stollen cake, 'Buttered brazils', Christmas puddings in July. 'It's a bit different,' she would say, with eyes brightened by her memory of childhood hunger. No more watering the milk; no more fried eggs cut in two. Though to the end of her life, Mum could never throw food away. The fridge always concealed a secret, that once she had been poor: at the back of shelves, little saucers with shrunken dark remnants of meals that would never be eaten, ten peas cratered like moons, one shrivelled parsnip, a half-inch of liver.

And I wonder, too late, looking back, whether all the newfangled pickled and spiced and sugared concoctions which Mum fell upon delighted, dry-roasted, cook-chilled, marinated – might have had something to do with the cancer that killed her.

But before the final reckoning was drawn up for my parents, there was time for years of 'lux', and some real luxury, brought to their feet by the river of age. Thanks to the Travel Club of Upminster (bless you, oh Travel Club of Upminster, now deceased, which flew plane-loads of pensioners off to the sun), Vic and Aileen found they could spend January and February abroad. As my father's neck grew stiffer and his fingers more knotted, as his pounding pace faltered and shortened into the small-stepping shuffle of Parkinson's, as my mother's right shoulder began to ache, they longed for warmth, for the winter in Norfolk is harsh, with winds coming straight from

Siberia and not much cover, on their little modern road with its newly planted, slow-growing shrubs. Then through one or other of their new coevals, their new classmates, they heard you could spend the winter in Portugal, land of almond blossom and beach-cafés, for less than the cost of your normal central heating. Moreover, 'in four or five-star hotels! Including meals!' They could hardly believe what they were telling us.

Five-star hotels. Did the skinny seventh of a seventh of a seventh ever dream she would get to stay in a luxury hotel with a balcony over the beach, not for a week but for months? As Vic became weaker and his glaucoma worsened, they were whisked not long after Christmas by the local taxi from their bungalow all the way to Gatwick, then into a disabled buggy that carried them painlessly all the way to their plane. Taxis. Airports. So far from the streets they were born in. My mother, who had always been frightened of flying, decided not to be. She was a pragmatist: 'What's the point of being frightened? You have to get on with it.'

But sometimes there's good reason to be frightened. In 1990, Mum must have repressed her fear and her sense that something was wrong, as all her life she had repressed her emotions, tried to placate and please. She was a long way from home, amongst the almond blossom, with the balcony over the strip of beach and the blazing sea, taking the same dazzling walks every day, the same question waiting when they came back to the room. She had only her husband with her, with whom her habit was concealment. When her digestion became more erratic, there were other things she could blame: the hotel kitchens, eating too much or too little, the heat. Constipation, then diarrhoea. 'I'm fine.' But then she was home and the evidence was undeniable, brutal, she could feel it, hard, in her abdomen. Now she had to tell. 'Vic, I've found a lump.'

But I don't have to tell that story, not yet. I don't have to see it all happen again. In life it came too fast, in this book I can keep her with me, my beloved mother, until her loss can be borne. And

I have to remember (because tragedy sits heavier in the scale-pan than everyday contentment) that she told me, more than once, during those last Norfolk years of retirement, 'I like my life, Marg. I hope you know I like my life. And when it's just Dad and I, we get on fine.' When the children were there, Dad was more 'on edge', she explained, 'although you know he loves to see you'.

But she said, 'I like my life.' How many people can say as much? And she said something else as well, when asked. 'After I went back, he never hit me again.'

There were things she could add up as triumphs. She drove the car (they got their first car in 1970, when they were both in their fifties; this in itself was a triumph); passed her test, to Dad's fury and disbelief, before he did; as his eyes declined, she became for the last few years the only driver. Mum in the driver's seat! She was a star in her creative writing class, popular for her quick wit, her one-liners, her Church gift for telling jokes. (Rarer in women, this talent bypassed me and went straight to my daughter. My husband says, 'You're funny but you can't tell jokes,' which is true; I can never remember the punch line, nor indeed the beginning.) She got her degree, her BA, from the Open University, aged sixty-four, and that mattered enormously to her. And the books she read for the politics and society modules filled her with indignant delight, fuelling the growing socialism she hid from her husband.

Why? Because she could not let him think the Gees had won the ideological battle. I remember sitting with her in the sunny kitchen-diner where Mum and the rest of the family always gathered while Vic presided alone in his red velvet Parker-Knoll armchair in 'the front room' next door, drinking crimson Ribena, often in a wine-red woollen waistcoat, mostly out of earshot though every so often he would call through, 'What was that, Aileen?' Mum was full of excitement about an article she was reading for her Open University course that told her the numbers of barristers, judges, top civil servants and cabinet ministers who came from public schools. 'Eighty-five per cent,' she announced to me happily, green eyes flashing across the kitchen table, smiling as if it was tremendous news; reinvigorated by this insight into a bad old world where nothing much had changed since she was small and poor – except that she and Vic and their children and other families like ours, by a miracle, thanks to the war and the welfare state and in particular free education, were no longer at the bottom of the heap, no longer poor, no longer working-class. 'Can you believe it, eighty-five per cent!'

'What was that Aileen?' came through the tiny hall, past the two open, flimsy doors, his voice weaker with the Parkinson's but still insistent, reluctant to lose its grip.

'Nothing, Vic.'

There's a saying, or maybe a song, 'Lucky if you don't get old before you get dead.' Not true of my parents. They were lucky to get old, if not very old, because age was a destination, a place they could go as of right and be welcomed. Somewhere they could finally arrive. Another class, kinder and more comfortably furnished, offering them at last a respite from climbing the hill, and from pushing their children on. A narrow ledge in the light, before it went out; a small warm plateau.

8   My animal luck (iv)

What do children need?
(parents)

Yes, parents. Since rights, really, are a luxury, a fiction, that's all biology insists we have: parents. Egg and sperm, conjoined. And to be allowed to be born.

So really I am asking something different – what do children need to have a chance of happiness? What do they need to live their lives?

And 'parents' is still the answer. My parents, for all their difficulties, for all the moments they gave us of worry, and pity, despite the pressures and even the fear, were all the parents that I needed. They loved me greatly. I never doubted that. They loved all three children, 'you kids' – and always put us first. My father was really a frustrated artist, with the darkroom he loved where he developed large black-and-white photographs, some of them stunningly bold and good, but a time had come after the war when he had to make choices. Photographer or teacher? He chose the steady job, teaching, because he put his family first. And with that choice came some of the deformations of his character from which we suffered.

Children of course need space, food, water, the animal necessities, which most of them get, in the developed world. They need food that isn't too faddy; so far as possible, they need foods that children have always eaten, because new ideas tend not to last. Skimmed milk, for instance, was the fad of my time; 'healthy' margarine of my mother's. She changed over to Flora because it was better for us. Years later, we discovered it wasn't. Just as we discovered, a few years ago, that whole milk contains more fat-soluble vitamins, more essential fatty acids, all things children need. My daughter had been drinking semi-skimmed milk, along with her parents, for most of her childhood. Sorry, Rosa.

Breast milk is so obviously best for babies that the success of formula milk is astonishing, after a hundred thousand years in which *Homo sapiens* raised their young without it. Not so astonishing, of course; formula milk frees women to work outside the home, which means, in the modern world, she can help feed the rest of her family. But breast must be best for the babies, except in those cases where the mother just can't. (Not fair to blame the babies, though. How many times did I hear in clinics, 'He won't latch on properly,' 'She doesn't seem to suck.') With enough time, and not too much pressure, for the great majority of mothers and babies, it will happen.

What helped me? My mother, coming with my father to the University College Hospital bed on Christmas Eve, the day after Rosa was born, saw me ineptly nuzzling her to my hard dry breasts, swinging her from one side to the other, with exhausted arms, and said, with a delighted smile, 'Isn't she doing well?' to my father. 'Oh, Margaret, you are doing well.' Which made me feel I was doing all right, and helped me stumble on till we found our own way, Rosa and I, as we fell in love, which with luck is what parents and babies do. Mum did what a parent should: she encouraged.

What didn't help me was the hospital. In those days they had charts, which seems unbelievable now, that all mothers had to fill in, with a column for 'LH' and a column for 'RH', twenty minutes each side, to be ticked five times a day. Insane. Fortunately, there were a lot of mothers, all lying around annoying the nurses, so no one noticed I wasn't doing it right. Rosa and I took much longer than that, and always did, for the nine months I fed her. If she had a long feed, she was perfectly contented, and at around four months, began to do something glorious afterwards, something which, in retrospect, looked forward to the teenage years when she began to sing: she produced, this little scrap of a thing, unable to talk, of course, or crawl, a sound we called her 'milk song', a humming, silvery sound that soared and dipped, tiny and pure, angel music. The sound of perfect happiness. In a few months, the song had gone. But Rosa and I had our animal bliss.

(After writing that paragraph, I worry. Of course I only write it because I *did* breast-feed, it worked for me, we were both happy. If I had not been able to, as might well have happened, for at one point my nipples became so painful that I had to use, briefly, an anaesthetic spray that is now no longer legal – sorry, Rosa – I would see things differently, would take the practical line about babies surviving perfectly well on formula milk – which of course, they do. Advice, advice. How pleasant to give it. But taking it's like eating pellets of paper.)

Children do need parents, and an animal life. A chance to climb and run and play out of the house, somewhere where the parents don't know what they are doing. A chance to take some manageable physical risks, so they can find out for themselves how far they can go. But my father banned ballet, which would hurt my feet, skating and roller-skating (risk of falling over), horse-riding (risk of falling off), tree-climbing, unless in Grandpa Gee's apple-tree (risk of falling down and breaking neck), Girl Guides (risk of uniforms and fascism), bike-riding (risk of road accidents), pets (risk of bites, scratches, infection), make-up and layer-cuts (risk of sex), walking on my own (risk of sex and murder), sitting in the sun (risk of sunburn), too much reading (risk of myopia), bed after 7.30 (risk of insomnia), television (risk of ideas from America). I was over-protected to a great degree, so my happiest memories of the years between nine and fourteen, the years when children should be starting to explore the world and test out their abilities, are all to do with times when my father had no idea what I was up to.

The risks of blanket prohibition should be plain. If parents know about something, they can mitigate the dangers; if children tell them nothing, they are in the dark. I don't think it occurred to Dad that we would defy him, although he always told us to think for ourselves. I put this suggestion into practice.

I was allowed to play in people's houses, whither I would be accompanied, and later collected. In point of fact, few people asked me, probably from a sense that our family was different, in a village where most people had lived for generations – the Toppers, the Muggeridges, the Aylings – and where nearly all children had to go, in the end, to the school where my father was head. In any case, raven-haired, freckled Pat Brewer asked me to her house, which was down past the station, not so modern as ours, part of a little row. Pat had a younger sister, and her mother was a flushed, kindly woman. Pat said we would go and play in the woods. 'I'm not allowed to,' I said – and followed her.

So began a magical, terrifying time when we excited and frightened ourselves half to death. Daux Wood had a typical Sussex ecology, a mix of bushes and saplings and big stag-headed oaks, with smaller hawthorns and silver birches and sandy, chalky clearings full of bluebells. We ran across the half-expected hazards: couples having sex in the long grass, vaguely-seen, because we turned our heads away and hurried on, flashes of white and wet red against the darkness which made us giggle and choke as we ran. The real fascination lay in going on further, piercing the thickets of brambles and bracken, pushing on after the paths had nearly all petered out. If you did so – with no idea of how you had come, so we never knew if we'd be able to find it again – you suddenly came to a patch of half-cleared heathland, slightly higher than the rest, hemmed in by forest.

I suppose, though recreating childhood distance is hard, it was a hundred yards square, or maybe less. Whenever we found it, it looked slightly different. Sometimes we seemed to see men, on their own, frightening men in drab brown macks, or men we allowed ourselves to think frightening, and perhaps, in fact, there was only one. The area was protected by a barbed wire fence which hung disconsolately in broken loops. We named it – probably I named it, since I was the child in love with names – the May Islands, after the regular circular bushes of hawthorn (also called 'may') round the perimeter, which were yellow-creamy-white in the month of May, and had the sweet, poisonous smell of danger. Once I broke some off and took it home to my mother, lying 'Pat's Mum sent you flowers from her garden.' But the petals were already falling like dust, and my mother said, 'May in the house is unlucky,' which added to my triumphant sense that the place where they had come from was criminal and sinister. Often we ran away as soon as we glimpsed the line of yellow bushes, unable to stand the tension any more.

But once at least, we went much further. At the centre, almost invisible from the edge, there were some long low buildings with shuttered windows, half-buried in the ground, with flat corrugated roofs, a spooky, deserted, inexplicable place with a notice whose lettering was painted out. Once something moved behind a half-darkened window and we ran, scraping our knees, twisting our ankles, for home. We built stories around it; we became secret agents. We could not stay away, though we could hardly bear to be there. In my mind the strange, sickly beauty of the hawthorn blossoms became confused with a sense of sin, the fact that Pat and I were risking our lives, the man, or men, we had seen or not seen, the hot-faced couples crushing the grass. I was nine, nearly ten, Pat was ten, nearly eleven, we were both on the verge of adolescence, and for both of us, for the whole of one spring, Daux Wood was the best place we had ever been.

In the end I could not resist telling my mother. She looked worried and said, 'There used to be a prisoner-of-war camp in there.

You shouldn't go there. It's trespassing.' She told my father, and that was that. No more visits to the Brewers.

But children need fun, and adventures. They need to find the borderlands of what is forbidden. After Pat had faded, Janet Gray became my friend, and was my 'home' best friend for the next ten years, until life sent me to university and her to a nurses' training college. One of the best things about Janet, apart from her love of running and her malleable nature, her kindness to me and her perfect small nose and her tomboyishness, which matched my own, was that her house was the total opposite of mine, full of people, noisy, easy-going. As usual, with very close relationships, there were psychic similarities, too, about our families.

For a start, she, like me, had two brothers, one real and one step, Graham and Dennie. Her stepfather, Reg Leadbetter, a farmhand whose work had given them the house, a big square tied cottage on Billingshurst High Street, would sometimes put his foot down; he seemed strange and old, wiry and weather-beaten, hard to understand with his strong Sussex accent, but he grinned at me, gappily, amiably enough, though once when I stayed one night too many I heard him in the bedroom: 'When's that gal going?' Whereas Janet's mother Renee (it rhymed with 'beanie') was adorable, a pushover. I love her still. I see her in the white overall she wore to work in the old people's home, her big toothy smile and shallow chin, always pleased to see me, often laughing, short black wavy hair streaked with grey. Kind to me. Loving to Janet. (What do children need? Kindness. Love.) There was a box of chocolates always open in the kitchen, and luscious white bread, forbidden at home. At Christmas, a row of bottles of sweet drinks. They had a small steep garden and a kind of shed where the boys were often doing something with bikes. In the front room the TV was always on. There was a huge dark sofa, into which you sank, and sat in a row in contented silence. Dennie wore leathers and had shiny black hair which he combed in a quiff, and was very handsome, more raffish and less academic than Janet's real brother, Graham, a gentle, humorous boy who played football. Of course I was in love with both of them, which neither noticed, so all was well.

The forbidden had to do with the bikes. Unable to learn to ride because of my father's obstinacy, I had done it, in the end, with frantic speed, on my cousin Sue's bike on Wolverton Rec (pronounced Wreck; I didn't know it was short for 'Recreation Ground') when we were at my grandparents, on holiday. I remember the bike: small, bright turquoise. Perhaps Uncle Lloyd had painted it. And the giddy feeling: cycling furiously forwards, having finally got up the speed to keep going, riding wildly on, unable to steer, unable to stop, until I fell off. I was probably about eight or nine when I learned, and I had had no practice since.

That didn't matter. Janet had plans for us. 'Let's cycle to the sea,' she said one Saturday. How did she know how to get to the sea? The sea was twenty miles away, and the road already had heavy traffic. 'We've got a spare bike.' They had; but the brakes were dreadful, and there was no suspension. As a total amateur, I did not notice this. Hurray! For not noticing, for no health and safety! Hurray for two teenagers biking to the sea!

I remember the snacks: Bourneville chocolate and peanuts, and freewheeling downhill, queen of the world, a tiny Janet flying on ahead of me, with round green fields on either side, cool sunny air blowing back my hair and the smooth whizzing sound of the chain for music, unable to brake, soon going so fast that the impetus carried me half-way up the next one – fortunately, as most hills defeated me, and Janet had to wait while I trotted up behind her. The bike had no gears, and the tyres needed pumping, and one of the handgrips was nearly worn away, but it opened up the world, it made us girls heroes, proved we could do more than our parents had told us.

Oddly, I don't remember if we got there. If we did get there, what did we do? I think it was Seaford, and we were tired, and had one portion of chips between us, and rested our aching calves on cool sand. But it was the riding away that mattered.

What else do children ideally need? Alasdair Gray once wrote that all children need is two adults who cohabit in relative amity. In which case, I didn't get what I needed, and nor do a lot of other children. I haven't always given it to Rosa, either. Nick and I love each other to distraction, but the distracted don't always get on. We are over-reactive, mercurial, rash. When trouble comes, it's hard to stay calm. I rage and he sulks, or he rages, and I'm fearful, but because of my history, I have to shout back, lest I turn into my quiet, frightened mother. Then something shifts, and we are laughing and tender. Sorry, Rosa, again, for the tropical storms. Though I hope you've never had to fear your father would murder your mother, which was my fear, as a child.

Standards. I do believe children need standards, even as something to rebel against. Not that I like the word 'standard', which sounds, well, too *standard*. But the other sense of 'standard' works for me: a flag held up against the blue, a watchword to remember when there are hard times. Nick's mother told him this: 'Always be kind, always be faithful, always be true.' When my whole career started to crumble before me, a friend of mine, not a very close one but a woman I had always liked, said, 'This is when character tells.' That was bracing. But I think it had such an effect because it took me back to things I had been taught as a child, most of them by my father: *Never give up. Have some backbone.* The Gees were too free with moral precepts, yes; but sometimes moral precepts can help.

There are useful absolutes. Do your best. *Don't steal, don't cheat, don't tell on people.* They are ropes to hold on to in trouble. When parents from my own generation, liberal baby-boomers all, tell me they feel morally at sea with their kids – 'you can't preach to them, their world's so different' – I think, is it really so different? Children need their parents to have some expectations, or else they will push, and push, and push, to see if there are any boundaries at all, and sprawl on their faces when nothing is there.

Hope. Children need hope. Should parents, 'being honest', diminish their hopes? 'He's hopeless at cricket, just like me.' 'I'm afraid that Alfie is a klutz at the piano, he takes after his father and mother.' Smiling charmingly at their own deficiencies, but also miring Alfie in them. To the child: 'For heaven's sake put down those plates, you're only going to drop them again.' To you, as the family arrives at your house: 'I'm sorry that Sally can't say hallo properly, it's not that we haven't taught her any manners.' Neither you nor Sally had noticed this gaffe, but the parent is terrified you will judge them. To their son, who has a plan: 'Don't waste your money on buying a guitar, you'll only give up, like you did with the recorder.' To an adult who is showing interest in the child: 'It's not worth asking her a question about that, she won't have anything interesting to say.' I have heard them all, wincing for the child. Nearly always, the parent is projecting their own failings on to the children, not seeing that others don't look at children simply as culpable extensions of the parents. So they pass on cruel judgements that were probably made about themselves, a lifetime ago, by their own parents. But children need not to be publicly judged by their parents. If it happens too often, they believe the judgements.

Bigger despairs can be passed on. Children have a right not to despair of their world.

When I was just eight, our teacher, Mr Norris, addressed the whole junior school together, which wasn't hard, for in the tiny village school at Watersfield, all the over-fives were in the same classroom. He had thin sandy hair and a bird-beak nose and that morning his voice was more serious than usual. I think it was November 1956. Perhaps Mr Norris didn't have a family; perhaps, that day, he needed one. He looked across us, we plain village children whose ages stretched between five and eleven; he must have seen the usual round pink faces, the unlined brows that understood nothing; the people with whom he spent his days. Smells of fart and fidgeting. And then out of the window at the sunny, chilly playground fringed with yellowing willows, then the blank water meadows.

'The next few days', he told us, slowly, 'will decide if the world will go to war. Planes are already in the air ...' That is all I remember of the speech that followed, and all it needed to infect me with terror.

In fact, the Suez crisis was ratcheting up into its worst phase. Israel had just invaded Egypt as part of a Franco-British deception. Russia was threatening reprisals. But none of us children knew anything of this. I had gathered from reading the *Daily Herald*, the more basic of the two papers we took, that there were bad people called communists, who sometimes pretended not to be, so every so often they had to be unmasked, often in things called unions. Those were the days of reds under the beds. I knew that Russia was our enemy. Suez, though, was a blank to me.

But war – the next days would decide if the world would go to war. Russia was somehow involved in it. For children who'd grown up, as all of us had, in the immediate shadow of World War Two, whose fathers had fought in it, and come back changed, who had heard their parents talk about the war a thousand times – if 'war' was mentioned by our head teacher, that meant the thing behind the shadow would come back, the terrifying thing we had all escaped by inches. War meant death. War was the end.

And indeed, things must have looked black to Mr Norris and other grownups at the time. I know now that American air defence – NORAD – had been told that unidentified aircraft were flying over Turkey, a hundred Soviet bombers were in the air, a British bomber had been shot down over Syria, the Soviet fleet was on the move. These 'facts' had moved forward contingency plans for a NATO nuclear strike against Russia.

Actually not one of the 'facts' was true, messy and dangerous though the Suez crisis was. The 'unidentified aircraft' were a flight of swans, the British bomber had a mechanical fault, NATO, on balance, preferred not to strike, the world was not about to end.

But I watched the skies, and thought about dying. Watersfield was on the flight-path to Gatwick. For the next few days, every plane that flew over was the one that would bomb us to smithereens. There was a constant ache of fear, which peaked when the hum of a plane began, a nagging presence growing slowly louder. Night-times were the worst, lying in bed and listening to the drone of distant engines.

What did Mr Norris think he was doing? Why did he want to frighten us? What point is there in telling children of evils that they are too small and powerless to do anything about? I sometimes think one reason for the apocalyptic streak that runs through so many of my novels might be the burden of terror Mr Norris gave me, which lingered long after the crisis went away. (But before I blame him for too much, I must ask why terror came to me so easily. I had seen my father trying to fight with my grandfather, rolling up his sleeves; 'Come out and fight me.' I had seen my mother crying in the kitchen. So the nerves and networks for fear were established. I did not have that 'relative amity'.)

Children need hope. Deserve to have hope. The world will muddy it soon enough, so if adults can, they should leave children unclouded. Apocalyptic global warming has not yet happened. Should children be taught it is inevitable?

There were times in my childhood when I had no hope, when my whole mental landscape was choked with fear ...

The cause of the original, primal terror was crumbs on a pale carpet. My brother John had dropped crumbs from his plate in Grandpa and Grandma's front room, which was only used for special occasions. I believe that Uncle Lloyd and Aunty Hilda had come round, with their children Sue and Martyn, for 'elevenses', so perhaps there was some degree of competition about the behaviour of the children. Poor John managed to spill his crumbs (it was the only carpeted room in the house; the others had lino, with bright rag rugs that Grandma made; carpets were rare, and mattered). Indulgent to his first and favoured grandson, Pa leaped up and got the carpet-sweeper, a modern innovation, in those days, working on rollers, like a very small, silent vacuum cleaner. But my father had told John to pick the crumbs up. 'I've told him to clean it up himself,' Dad said. 'John will pick them up, he has to learn.' 'Well this is quick and easy,' Pa insisted, advancing on my father with the carpet-sweeper. *'No, he has to learn.'* A full-blown confrontation had come from nothing. 'I'll pick them up,' said John, as eager as everyone was to avoid trouble.

But trouble could not be avoided between these two fathers fighting over one son. Soon Pa had said the unforgivable. Apparently yielding, but in fact planting in my father's breast an unbearable barb, he said, 'Well, Vic, we won't argue. You're John's tyrant.' Though he said the word 'tyrant' as though it was neutral, though the *form* of what he said was yielding the point, there was bitter gall in the content. And my father, maddened like the bull he was, a heavy man compared to his father's neat, dancing gadfly, groaned, 'Tyrant? I'm not a tyrant. I'll ... Come outside, Pa. I'll fight you.'

(And of course, the bitterness came from the irony. Pa himself, in his time, had been a tyrant. He was now indulging his grandson as he had never indulged his son.)

That morning of the year when I was six, I believed that the world was going to end. I remember every detail, half a century later. I watched Grandpa follow Daddy into the Peale Road garden. An unspeakable horror was coming upon us.

But then, through tears, I saw something else: Grandpa was pulling and patting at my father's arm, not hitting him, trying to calm him down. 'Don't take on, Vic, don't take on.' The bomb didn't fall. The war didn't happen. The men, in the end, did not fight each other, we did not leave for home, as my father threatened, and the battle blew over, with much pain, and Grandma grey-faced, sitting clutching her chest.

Did the adults understand what it meant to us children? It is happening still, in the blaze of white light as the back door opens and they lurch into the garden.

I can only gauge how it weighed on me from my memory of the next time we went to Wolverton. That we were going to go back, after such dreadful events, had oppressed me since my mother had mentioned it. We had been with my father's school, Watt Close, on a foreign exchange trip to Holland. I loved the holiday; the hotel had a swimming pool with big rubber rings, and chocolate milk. There were wide red and yellow fields of tulips, and a stormy barge trip on the Zuider Zee. But as the days went by, the fear began. We were going to Wolverton as soon as we got back. I prayed that the holiday would never end.

I was incapable of stopping time. I was powerless in the grip of my family. Inexorably, we got to the day when we were off the boat, and on the train in to Euston, the station where we always changed when we were on our way to Grandpa and Grandma's. The glass of the window, which I pressed my head against to feel the almost pleasant pain of the train jolting, was hard and offered me no help. Raindrops ran in jerky streams down the glass, hanging fire, immobilised, till heavy as tears, then splitting when you least expected it into a slick sprinting delta of water. I tapped the pane, smeared it, desperate to affect them; they carried on endlessly, uninterested. But then I remembered an idea I had had when I was falling asleep in the hotel in Holland. Of course, I could simply stop breathing. If you wanted to die, you could simply stop breathing. I could not stop time, but I could die, quite easily, and never have to go to my grandparents' again. I tried it, cautiously; it wasn't too bad. I was sure that by the time I gasped air back in, I was almost dead, it was almost done. My spirits lifted. I was six years old, and cheering myself with thoughts of suicide.

In that way, and at that moment, I would say, looking back, I must have lacked something children need to live. I do not blame my family. *They could not help it.*

But once again, nothing happened. We went back to Wolverton. Everyone was nervous. Pa and Vic made an effort to get on. We spent more time at Stony Stratford than usual, and in the evenings, sat and surrendered to the soothing authority of 'Dixon of Dock Green' on the black-and-white television. My second and third attempts to stop breathing were in any case a great deal harder than my first. It was something, of course, I could not fully rehearse. And I needed not to know that my escape route didn't work.

What do children need? For life to go on. Somehow the wounds scabbed over, the rawness disappeared. We got over the horror, as families must. Given time, both body and mind can recover, as long as no one has actually gone beyond hearing, beyond reparation, as long as no one has died.

More and more I think that only life matters. That the embryo, though its life will not be perfect, be allowed to cling on. Allowed to be born. That the quarrelling adults don't murder each other.

I managed to grow up with two living parents. All over the world, children long for that. And having had it, I can't complain.

9 I leave home

I do not leave home

i

I was a very immature seventeen. I was hideously unready to leave home. Socially, sexually, emotionally, practically. I had never had a boyfriend, never had sex, never had a job except six days' currant picking, with Janet, on a local farm. I had never been out in the evening. I could not drive, sew, cook, shop or clean; could not manage money or social life.

I was clever, though, and had read a lot, and was as desperate to get out as I was unready.

I was also in the middle of my only ever breakdown, though I didn't realise it till decades later.

My last year at school was eventful. In the month that I was seventeen, I sat Oxford and Cambridge entrance, the only girl to do so from Horsham High School, sitting alone in the stuffy prefect's room, my pen flying over the paper. The exams, in those days, were general essays, which gave you a chance to show off a bit, plus a translation paper, which was my idea of bliss – I loved French and Latin with cerebral passion. Then I was called to interview. This was much more taxing: what to wear, what to say? I would have to talk to strangers, which I was not used to. Dad did not let strangers into the house. Mum and I went to Horsham, once again to Chart and Lawrence, the only clothes shop that there was, and bought a 'good suit', a russet brown, wide-gauge, corduroy suit with a curved half-belt on the double-breasted jacket. It was purest chance that it was in stock. Lined in rust-brown silk, it was expensive, but Oxbridge interviews were important. Vic's pride, Vic's money, bought it for his daughter.

I wasn't totally sure it was me. Wasn't it, well, a tad sensible? Didn't I want to be Bohemian? (Not that I knew what Bohemian was.) I wore it with a black nylon polo neck sweater and my black intellectual squared-off glasses. Not a bad look, now I think about it, and I must have appeared more mature than I was.

But at Cambridge, naïvety and ignorance told. I was interviewed at Newnham by a Mrs Leavis, a name that meant nothing to me. She opened the door with a yapping white dog which made my fear intensify. I was unused to dogs. Dad had forbidden them. It yipped and leaped and smelled damply alive, distracting me when I needed to think.

(Would it bite my fingers? I dared not pat it. I became a bundle of naked fingers.) Mrs Leavis herself was also, in my memory, small, white-haired and puggish in appearance, with a crop of white hair that matched her dog's. Her room was large and dark. She did not seem to like me. What would I prefer to talk about? Innocently, I volunteered 'Keats', not knowing that her husband, the god-like FR Leavis, had published a major 're-evaluation' of Keats. (I must have *heard* of FR Leavis, but it wouldn't have occurred to me that they were related, that critics had wives, and dons had dogs. For me, the world of books was so far from the real one, where real people lived in boxes, in Billingshurst.) I rambled effusively about the poet while the dog barked and Mrs Leavis looked stern. Which secondary sources had I read? The names I cited did not include 'Leavis'. Time slipped away. I was drowning in words. Her questions were sparse and irritable. My suit and polo neck were very hot. At last, thank God, she had heard enough. By then, I was drenched with sweat under my layers. When I came out and reported to my fellow candidates, the more knowledgeable ones were aghast. Hadn't I heard of QUEENIE LEAVIS? You *talked about Keats*? You *didn't*!

At Oxford, however, things went better. These interviews were spread over a whole weekend. Once again, some girls had inside information. For example, a thrilling rumour spread that we were all up for entrance awards. I remember the drunken feeling of pleasure, spreading through my veins like adrenalin, followed swiftly by unease. This phenomenon has shadowed me all my life; a path to glory opens, then I am afraid. An emptiness starts to spread in my ego when it is inflated by something outside, something that is not part of my essence. *Something is overtaking me.*

Did it mean I would have to be clever for ever? Would I have to go on jumping through hoops, a never-ending tunnel of flaming hoops? Would I lose my self in the lights and the noise? My secret self, who liked bikes and clouds, a silent happiness which could not be destroyed – unless I let myself be lured away.

I was letting myself be lured away.

Who was I really? Should I be here? I was trying to please my parents and the teachers, as I too often tried to please. Doing it had brought me to this strange hall, these long dark tables lined with fluting girls. Did I belong with these flower-like sophisticates, in these elegant buildings with their endless corridors? (They seemed elegant to me, but this was before I saw the older, richer, men's colleges. I thought all the girls had come from private schools; some had, of course, but some were frightened, like me. Some of them were probably spotty, and plain.)

Yet I had been a child who liked to win races and come top in school exams. Part of me, coarser, hungrier, longed to do well, burned to do well. Part of me was competitive, and this was a bigger, better competition. (Yet burning, surely, meant you were in hell.) And these were interviews, not honest competitions. I was going to need social skills, alas. In social matters, I was utterly unskilled, though my ego couldn't wait to go out and bat.

All social situations, then, led to shame. I was horribly aware of getting things wrong; sometimes at the actual moment when my foot, with aberrant energy, lurched into my mouth, but always during the replays, and I was never short of replays. I made one gaffe I still blush to think about. Miss Woolf, the medieval specialist, was entertaining another proto-Scholar and me to sherry. It was evening; the general atmosphere was congratulatory. Though nothing was spelled out, the rumour was true, we were being considered for awards. But the other proto-Scholar was more charming than me, livelier, prettier, more graceful. I wanted to show I had gravitas, or wanted, perhaps, to say something, anything, probably grandiose with sherry, which I don't suppose I had drunk before (I hate my young self: I pity my young self.) Something enormous burst out of my mouth. 'Are there opportunities to do research?' I had levered myself into the light conversation, sounding Germanic and oppressive. They were looking at me. The only way was forwards. 'I would like to do – like to do – a *doctorate*.' My ambition thwacked down on to the subtly shaded carpet. It sat there like a great pie, unwanted, a pink pork pie lobbed in through the window. My fellow proto-Scholar giggled charmingly, and raised and lowered her mobile dark eyebrows. Her mouth was full, her teeth were white. A gulf yawned before me. Then Miss Woolf replied.

Her response may not have been scornfully meant, and yet it seared me to the core. 'Ah yes, ah well, it's perhaps a little, just a little *early* to be thinking about that,' she said. 'We would normally, ah, look at the performance of undergraduates at, ah, a *much later* stage, before we *invite them* to do research.'

I could not sleep that night for reliving the moment. I had been what my father would call conceited. Had I even been what he would call swollen-headed? I lay awake till light scored the heavy curtains and flooded the strange unfriendly room. Why was I here? I felt large and empty. I would never sleep, my shame was too great.

And yet, when I told this story to my husband, he could not

understand why I was embarrassed. 'It was a perfectly ordinary question. Have you really felt ashamed of it all your life?' The sad answer is, 'Yes'. The healthy response would probably have been to realise that Oxbridge dons have a way of sounding snotty. Perhaps my unease is also explained by the inchoate sense I had, even then, that this might not be the right path. (I did do a doctorate in the end, and it took me away from my real writing, though the reading – Sterne, Fielding, Thackeray, Woolf, Beckett, Nabokov, Vonnegut – helped me to be a novelist.)

Two or three days later, in the Christmas holidays, a yellow telegram was brought to the door. It went something like this: CONGRATULATIONS STOP OFFER OF MAJOR OPEN CLOTHWORKERS' SCHOLARSHIP STOP PLEASE ACCEPT WITHIN TWO DAYS STOP SOMERVILLE COLLEGE OXFORD. My mother cried with joy, my father was triumphant. *Margaret had done it! Margaret had shown them!* All my doubts disappeared at once. It was one of the happiest mornings of my life, whatever I have said about my queasy ego, whatever mixed gifts Oxford would bring me. I held my yellow telegram and sat in the bay window, which was drenched with winter sunlight, listening to the music swelling from the wireless, which played for me, and spoke to me, which would carry me away from my dull modern house, my squabbling family, my little village. Nobody realised I had got away! Perhaps my quiet self is the self that writes, but there's poetry in success as well; in moments of glory; in watching the successful. They pass down the street, briefly touched with gold, though no one stays in the sun for ever. *To ride in triumph through Persepolis* ... the fate of Marlowe's Tamburlaine. That morning, I thought I saw Persepolis. I swam in the stream of joy from the wireless, 'M-y-y shi-i-p is coming in ... Baby baby, m-y-y sh-i-i-p is coming in ...'

Mrs Leavis cannot have entirely despised me, because Cambridge also offered me a place, but I accepted Oxford. I still had two more terms of school to go, and my A- and S-levels to take, though the scholarship was not dependent on them. I could get Cs and Ds if I liked. I was godlike. I was invulnerable.

Many a slip; I nearly fell to my death. I was clever, but of life I still knew absolutely nothing.

ii

That Easter my father led a school party on an exchange visit to St Aigulin in northern France. It was weeks before my A-levels, but I was studying French, and I'd have plenty of time to do revision. I did revision, but I also found I was attractive to the local male population. To them I was not 'Dobbin's daughter', nor that weird brainy girl who went to grammar school. Something marvellous, unprecedented, happened; I was taken up by the local group, the coolest boys, a foursome. My favourite boy was said to be 'un noble', Jean de something or other, thin and handsome, but all of them dressed well, in a '60s way, and rode tiny motorbikes with great style.

I worked for my A-levels every day, in the pretty upstairs room in the village inn where my family stayed, and in the evening, the boys took me out. Which literally meant 'out'. We walked around, talking, under summer evening skies, and they showed me their bikes, and rode up and down. After that they went to the village hall and practised their music, while I admired them. It was the beginning of the life I wanted, or so I thought, before it all went wrong. They were boys, and I had grown up with boys, my brothers, my father, my family of males. I was learning afresh that I liked them. It was utterly, completely, innocent.

But the minds of fathers of daughters are corrupted by fear, and suppressed desire, and by guilt about these feelings. My father must have seen I was starting to escape, right under his nose, and he could not bear it. He said I could go out, with an 11 pm curfew, but secretly he fumed and fretted. My mother warned me, but I only laughed. Dad had 'heard the boys talking in the street beneath their window'. My father's French was ludicrous, breaking down, when he spoke, within a couple of words, into loud, slow English. Nevertheless, he now claimed to understand it. 'He thinks he heard them saying "Elle est facile,"'my mother said. Was I hurt, or just contemptuous? Openly contemptuous (though only to my mother), secretly hurt, at a deep level. Mum knew as well as I did that the voice was in his head, the enraging voice saying, 'She's easy, she's anyone's.'

All the same, I should have listened to his fears, and I should have kept the curfew. One night I came back ten minutes late and was shouted at, which made little impression. Was I trying to annoy my father or (more likely) unable to explain my need to be back by eleven to my glamorous new friends? The next night I came back at eleven-fifteen, escorted by all four members of the group.

The moon was high: I remember that. I can still see the moonlit road before me, lined with trees, for we were in the country, the hotel ahead of us and on the left. We five young people were spread across the road, owning the road, laughing and happy, though I had a little undertow of worry – I was late, but surely, not very late. Then I saw my father, in the distance, hurrying towards me, down the middle of the road, a small hurrying figure; getting bigger; here. It wasn't easy to see his expression. My friends greeted him, in poor, polite English; he grabbed my arm, and wouldn't let it go; they left knowing he was in a rage, and turned tail, diminished, going back towards the village.

I do not remember the fifty metres we walked, yoked together by violence, back to the hotel. He did not hit me till we got inside, having pushed me upstairs and into my bedroom. I will never quite forgive him for what ensued (though I must forgive him; I must. I do. If I don't forgive him, it will never go away. After all, I was late, and he was terrified. Of what I had been doing, or what was being done to me.) He hit me by the window; I fell on the bed. He hit me, again and again, on the bed, inchoate with rage, inaccurate. On the arms and legs, on the side and shoulders, but I am pretty sure he also slapped my face. It would be consistent with behaviour I remember. And he shouted; *don't you have any self-respect?*

What was my mother doing while this went on? My memory after this point is hazy, but there is no doubt that she knew what was happening, because it later transpired that the whole hotel heard. I think I remember her coming in, afterwards, as I lay there swollen and furious with crying. 'Are you all right, Margaret? *Are you all right?*' Yes, my mother came in. I do remember. And I hated her as well, for not stopping him, for not protecting me, for being one of a two-parent system which did not see I was a separate person and had a right to be respected. (My father should have understood there is no self-respect without respect from others.) I rejected her; I hugged my bruises. (And now I wonder if my father sent her. He must have realised he had gone too far. Now my mother had to sort things out, as she had to sort out all family troubles. 'Aileen, go and see that she's all right.')

Next day was a nightmare. Life had to go on. We had to be seen in the hotel at mealtimes. The kind, attractive manageress stopped me on the stairs. Her face was serious. Was I all right? She was worried about me. It meant so much that another adult, not part of the family, bothered to tell me she was on my side, that something was wrong, that it wasn't just my wickedness. Yet I also remember how eager I was to reassure her. Of course it was all right, indeed it was nothing. 'Mais j'ai tout entendu,' she persisted, grave. *I heard everything.* But I felt ashamed. I couldn't get my father into trouble. Family came first. And it was all my fault. A large part of me felt it was all my fault.

The story I have just told is not the reason, the overt reason, for the breakdown I had. It was part of a pattern of behaviour I knew, only different because I was nearly an adult, and because it involved my sexual self so closely.

Lack of respect. That was what mattered. If only I had known enough to shout that back at him, when he was roaring that I lacked self-respect. What do children need? One thing daughters need from their fathers is respect for their sexual selves. Vic's fear and desire made him crash through the wall. Fathers would do well to think the best of their daughters (I had done nothing; neither kissed nor touched; there were four boys, not one, they were my knights, my cavaliers, and my father was a sad and violent man. Part of me hates him for it still, a part of me that I strain to outgrow. Because he was my father, and loved me very much. I was his first daughter; he had had no practice, and would never get a chance to play that evening better. His feelings were tidal, and he was helpless.)

But if fathers think the worst, the girls have nothing to lose. We have already, irrecoverably, lost our reputation.

Life returned to normal, more or less, the first time someone laughed, at our table. Then the grim lid of gloom lifted away, and I was glad enough to see it go. Three or four days later, the fair came to St Aigulin, the summer fair, the village's great event, which brought young people from all over the region. Perhaps inspired by guilt about what had happened, my father was almost eager for me to go. My curfew was extended to midnight. I remember what I wore, which I thought was high fashion, though it would only have made the grade in a French village: a knee-length, small red-and-black-flowered cotton dress, figure-hugging, with a Peter Pan collar, a short navy fitted jacket, which I soon took off, a long 'chain pendant', the metal indeterminate, which featured a many-armed Thai goddess, white fish-net stockings, navy heeled sandals. I felt like a chic seventeen-year-old, and for the French, I may have had that indefinable illusion of attraction that comes when one is seen as from somewhere else. I was the seventeen-year-old *anglaise*. It was a hot evening. We were all on heat.

I was escorted, as usual, by my four French friends. They had been warier, different since the scene with my father. They warned me about one thing: 'the boys from Bordeaux'. They weren't like the boys from St Augulin. I could trust the boys from St Aigulin, *évidemment* – obviously – but not the others who would come to the fair. I hardly listened, or believed they existed.

But the boys from Bordeaux really were at the fair, and you could pick them out by their knowing look, an air of slight loucheness, the cut of their jeans. My village group no longer seemed so cool. I saw a tall boy with tinted glasses, and he saw me, and perhaps he thought he could pick *me* out by *my* knowing look, for my father's insults had taught me one thing, I was sexual, and people were likely to want me. Whatever he saw, this boy liked me. He saw me on the dodgems, with one of my friends, and I saw him looking, and I looked back. I felt proud, and reckless; I expect I was still angry. I was nearly grown up, I was going to prove it. I could look after myself, couldn't I?

He was slim, with jeans and a flowered shirt. Soon we were on the dodgems together, then walking round the fair, arm in arm. He had full wet lips. I don't remember his name, but in his dark glasses he looked mature and gorgeous. Somehow I had left my foursome behind. If I had stayed at the fair they would have found me soon enough, but the Bordeaux Beau had other ideas. 'Let's go for a walk,' he said, and his arm was round my shoulders, hot and exciting, his fingers were stroking the back of my neck. Why not? I thought. It was a warm May evening, the sky was still bright with the afterglow, I would soon be eighteen, I could do what I wanted. Surely no harm could come to me? I can see us now, laughing and walking away, looking confident and conspiratorial. Even as we went I was picturing us, thinking, 'Here I am with a handsome man, people will be noticing, and wondering where we're going.' It added to the tingle of pleasure in my stomach. Nothing had happened to me before, except for Frank Lammas, at my father's school, and a beautiful boy, a Greek Cypriot, Dino, who'd kissed me at a party that New Year's Eve, to the strains of the Beatles' 'Michele'. But these were mere boys. Now I was with a Frenchman.

'Let me show you the house where I am staying. We could have a coffee, or a drink,' he said. That sounded attractive, and grownup. The house was small and white, detached, pleasant. There was no one at home. Did he give me a drink? Soon he was showing me upstairs. I wanted to go, there was no coercion. What did I expect to happen up there? I must have thought that we would kiss. Anything further was beyond my comprehension.

But soon we were kissing on the bed, and he was trying to take my clothes off. Without his shirt he looked lean and young, but without his dark glasses his eyes seemed crossed, and his tongue was enormous and slobbering. I was holding my dress down, and trying to explain. I still wasn't frightened, something to do, perhaps, with that vulnerable lazy eye, and the almost girlish fullness of his lips.

'Je suis vierge,' I said. *I am a virgin.* 'Montre-moi ton corps,' he replied, he begged. *Show me your body: show me, show me.* I heard noises in the house, and grew anxious; I didn't want to be discovered up there, perhaps by other French people, respectable French people, not from racy Bordeaux but St Aigulin. He was getting more insistent, and impatient. I resisted, and the kisses were too wet, and after a bit, became boring. He was much less attractive than he had been. I said I wanted to go home. He put on his glasses, but not his shirt, and left the room, saying, 'Wait a moment.'

And then the real terror began, because he did not return alone, but with a short, fat friend, greasy-looking and brutal. He had a thin line of moustache above his mouth, something alien, not youthful. 'Je suis conscrit militaire,' he said. *I am a soldier, a military conscript.* The tall one nodded, weak, upstaged. I wasn't going home. The conscript wouldn't let me. This weekend was his leave. He wanted to have fun. He was going to have fun. 'Or we will kill you.'

A sick shock of fear as the world turned over. My ribs and stomach crushed together with horror. The room was suddenly a hell, a prison.

I had been wicked, and now I would be punished. I had always known that one day I would be killed. Now it had come, the black centre of the nightmare.

The high bed was in the middle of the room, back to the wall, electric light to the left of the bed and overhead, horribly clear. To my right was a window I am sure was uncurtained, so the house cannot have been overlooked. Outside was the night sky, now almost dark, and the green countryside, and somewhere the village, distant lights under the bulging black trees on the horizon, and normal life, and the hotel, and *my parents*, who were waiting in ignorance for me to come back, and the future, the life that I might have had if I had not come to this small lighted prison. All of it impossibly far away, and I had left it behind for ever. I saw my own death; there was no way out. The tall boy went away, leaving the fat one, telling me he would soon be back.

Why was I immobilised by threats of violence? I think my father should answer that question. Our house had been ruled by threats of violence and actual violence, since we were small. He was not very violent, as these things go; he didn't have to be, the fear was enough. I never thought, as I would now, of fighting those men, of calling their bluff. Perhaps they would have been ashamed to punch me, as they were not ashamed to touch me when I didn't want them to. How deeply I was part of my difficult family is shown by the thoughts that ran through my brain like electric shocks, agonising, twitching: my parents would be angry. My father would be shamed. There would be a terrible, final scandal. Though I was facing death, I could still feel guilty.

But as I struggle to remember what actually happened that early summer night in St Aigulin, what that hateful, fat little man did to me, I realise one odd thing that makes me happy: I never considered giving in. Partly, of course, because I *was* a virgin. I simply wouldn't have known what to do, or which halfway houses it was tactical to offer. (And maybe, I think now, they didn't know either. They were Catholics, deep in the Catholic countryside, in 1966, when the pill was very new. Maybe having sex was not something they were used to.)

But killing he was keen on, the little conscript, keen on threatening it, at least, this olive-skinned, lard-faced, stubble-headed man so far from the tall pale handsome Frenchman I had thought, in the rosy glow of sunset, I was choosing. This one had no aura of youth or glamour. He did not smile under his creepy moustache, a black greasy millipede crawling on the sweat. He did not, like the first boy, try to woo me. He was fat and brutal and excited. I remember clearly asking him if he had a sister, or a mother. Perhaps he was wearing a crucifix. He would not admit to having either, he would not talk to me, I was just a body.

The title of this book is *My Animal Life*, and my feelings for animals are interest and respect, but I remember the dread thought: *he's just an animal.* For him I had no soul, no special livingness, no consciousness that had to be regarded. And so, in this hot prison, he abolished me – we abolished each other – so he could harm me. I didn't see sex: all I saw was death. There was nothing alive, just the end of the road. And that longed-for world outside the window. I do not know how long it went on. I know he didn't rape me, or damage me physically, he just repeated his dead ultimatum. I do remember that I was crying. And I remember I was praying, as well, small stumps of prayer: *please God. Please help me.*

And then the world turned. The story breaks, and pivots. The door swings open, and light pours in. My prayer is answered. *My prayer was answered.* It wasn't time; this was not the end. In another universe, perhaps, I died, but in this one, suddenly, I slipped my prison. The room was full of people – men – but they were shouting at the conscript, and he was shrinking, and I saw two faces I recognised, my friends from the village, come to find me. They took me downstairs, they were vocal and worried, they grouped around me, excluding the city boys, they found my jacket and my chain pendant, they made black coffee, which I never drank. I stopped crying as they comforted me. Unbelievably, I had been saved. It wasn't even late; long before midnight.

Someone took me back to the hotel. Blindly, I did as I had promised and popped my head into my parents' bedroom. From my father's point of view, nothing had happened, so long as I did what I was told, so long as I was back before my curfew. Had I had a nice time? Yes, I lied. A lovely time. All my friends had been there.

(And I still don't know what happened that night. Did the first boy, Lazy Eye with his dark glasses, panic about the rape he thought was in progress and go and find acquaintances from the village, where everybody knew each other? Did the house belong to someone from the village, sons whose parents were away, who came back by chance and stumbled on the story? It doesn't matter. Somehow I was saved.)

But the randomness of it has stayed with me for ever. I did not save *myself*, by initiative or courage, by strength or cunning or sexual know-how. I was saved by chance, or perhaps by prayers. I was helpless in the power of others. And the underside of that is, I needn't have been saved. A universe existed where I was not saved. It was terrifying, full of rape and murder.

I thought I had escaped, but I was only half-right. The school trip ended three days later. I did not say a word to my mother and father, though the story must have circulated in the village. One of my four friends, the boy I least liked, took me out one night and asked me too many questions: 'Mais qu'est-ce qu'ils t'ont fait, dis-moi, Margaret?' *What did they do to you, tell me, Margaret?* He wanted the details. Naïve though I was, I knew he was excited by the thought of what might have happened to me. I closed up tighter, like a clam.

A week or so after we got back home, my A- and S-level exams began. My mind responded; I sat down and did what I had always done, and did very well. Not long afterwards, the school term ended, and we all stood and cried as we sang the school song for the very last time, 'To serve is to reign', that hymn of the female downtrodden.

And then there was a blank. I did have a plan, to do my very first job, for the civil service, as a filing clerk in an office in Horsham. The job was very boring, and very easy, sorting grey-green cardboard files alphabetically. The pay, I think, was £1 or £2 a week (but then my rent, three years later, was only £3). Only two things were wrong: first, my fellow-workers. One was a stout, glossy-haired girl who had been at my father's school, and seemed friendly, and offered to take me under her wing. Her name was Thelma; she had a soft voice and a strong Sussex accent. She talked incessantly. Soon she was pouring pure vitriol, softly, constantly, into my ear. Whenever she could get me out of other people's hearing, she told me bad things about my father. 'It's going downhill, the school. He's losing his grip, everyone says so. Shall I tell you what we used to say about your father?' I was powerless, fascinated, by Thelma. I did not know how to deal with her, how to stop her talking, or stop myself hearing. I felt I saw evil, once again. And so the second thing went wrong: my mind. The world started to slide under a veil of terror.

Every lunchtime I escaped from the office, and Thelma, and bought myself chips from the fish-and-chip shop. They were huge and greasy and I could not eat them. There was a phone-box in the street outside. One day I rang up my mother in a panic. 'I hate this job. I can't go back.' She was puzzled, and consoling. I returned to Thelma.

Poor Mum. I phoned her, crying, every day that week. I did not know what was the matter. My father agreed I should give up the job. I think they told themselves it meant I was special; *Margaret wasn't meant for filing.* But giving up beached me in structureless summer, in the empty days before we went away on a camping trip, the last family holiday, tenting with my parents and my cousin Susan. Something definite: the holiday. But before that, a featureless glaze of time, and beyond, a cliff of anxiety, the beginning of Oxford, at the start of

October. The security of school and the prefects' room, of lying on the sunny garden bank with the girls, my friends, my dear friends who had grown up with me, Jill and Gillian, Jacky and Hilary, Patty and Lizzie and all the rest, that big gang of girls who looked out for each other, sprawled on the short yellow grass we loved under the monkey-puzzle tree outside the library window, giggling and teasing and dreaming of the future, was shrinking inexorably into the past. No more navy jumpers with gold at the neck, no more uniform days promising safety. I sat at home, in the new vacant summer, watching things float away from me. And everything turned blank and grey, a thick goo of slime that choked reality.

Worse, it *became* reality. Like other people suffering from depression (I had no idea I was depressed) I felt I at last saw what life was: an alternation of emptiness and terror. When I lay down to sleep, my heart beat madly, and I woke terrified, night after night. Then that fear invaded my days, as well. I tried to tell my mother, but I only cried, because I did not know what to tell her, I did not know what was happening, and couldn't make the connection that now seems obvious, between this terror and my untold story, the thing that had happened in St Aigulin and at once been suppressed when I reported to my parents: 'I had a lovely time. All my friends were there ...' Yes, watching me, afterwards, pale and worried, wondering if the conscript had raped me.

I don't believe in therapies that mean endlessly reliving traumatic events, but I know that I needed to talk to someone. If I had done, perhaps there would have been no breakdown. But physically, the scene had been left far behind, on the other side of a channel ferry, and nothing could be told without appalling my parents and causing – what? Anger, disapproval. So I kept it inside, and slid into paralysis.

It's forty years ago, more or less exactly, but I do not enjoy recovering this period, still feel it's somehow perilous. It has never happened to me again, but sometimes the terror has brushed against my cheek, often at night, like a bat's wing, passing, a leathery thing whispering of claws in the darkness, hissing that if you fall through the surface, there is nothing underneath, just falling for ever. I won't invite it to come near again.

As I said at the beginning of this chapter, 1966 was an eventful year. The good thing I learned, slowly, piecemeal, gathering it as inefficiently as fragments of gold from a dirty river, was that life will save you, if you let it. I saw no doctors, took no pills, talked to no one until years later. But grain by grain, second by second, I began to forget, to be distracted. One night the terror did not come, and I slept till morning with a steady heart beat, even though that was followed by twenty more nights of torment. There were mornings when I managed a couple of hours before the grey veil closed over the day. Then we went camping: there were lots of things to do. I had to be normal for my cousin, loving, cheerful, athletic Susan. We sang on walks and in the tent at night, and even though for me the song had lost its joy, performing it, filling my lungs and sounding the notes of 'My Favourite Things' in the clear blue air, made my body remember the feel of being happy, and my body started to save my mind. My animal body. My animal life.

What finally pushed me back into normality was leaving home. Of course, as I said, I was unready, but if I had stayed, I would never have been ready. I might have been disabled for life. What do children need? They need to leave home, even if home will always come with them. I was nervous, but in a different way, and that normal nervousness, that fear of gaffes, that intense busyness of the first term at Oxford, trying to make friends and fathom the system, going to lectures, joining clubs, slowly crowded out the blankness, the bat's feet, and made me so tired that I slept at night. Fear came back at Christmas, in my narrow bed, and less strongly in the vacations that followed. Was it the dreadful quietness of the Sussex night, without the happy cries of drunken young people? Was it the oppression of life at home?

And let's not forget the deep task of parents is to see that their children *can* leave home, are enabled to have a life of their own. My parents somehow made it possible. Even my father let me go. There are too many children who never leave. I left, ineptly. I was able to. Though if they had not pushed me so hard at school, I might have been older, and better equipped.

I see this chapter reads like an indictment of my father, and maybe it should. Maybe he deserves it. Maybe it's time to recite the charges.

But if so, I have to defend him too, because he is dead, and I am the writer.

I hated him, and yet we recovered. I recovered, and he recovered, and one day he would say 'Sorry' to me. My mother told me that after they had seen me off at Horsham for the train to Oxford with my vast brown trunk, hand-initialled by Vic in his over-careful lettering, M. M. GEE, my father came home, went straight into my bedroom, and cried for an hour, could not stop.

10 What do women need?

what do men need ?

I was nineteen years old when I first had full sex with a man, which seemed shamefully behindhand. I think we were all eager not to be virgins, we clever girls at Somerville, but men were not allowed to stay overnight, and college rooms had thin walls like eggboxes. So it couldn't really happen till I moved out of college. The man, also, had to be vaguely right, though the muddle and chaos of those times, and my life, is shown by the fact that to this day I am not quite sure which of two men first went 'all the way'. One seemed to get quite far up my way, and it didn't hurt, and felt fairly pleasant; I was glad it was happening at last; but then the second one went deeper, further, and I liked it, and him, a great deal better. On balance I decided the second was The First, and told him he was, and I think he felt betrayed when in the course of a quarrel a few years later I chose to announce it wasn't him after all. The truth was perhaps that a girl who's been a tomboy and done a lot of hurdles races at school has little physical virginity left.

I found I had no shyness about sex. It seemed perfectly natural and very exciting and I wanted to try out more of it. The fear I had felt that evening in France (which came back again when on two more occasions I was physically attacked by strangers, once in Italy, once outside my house in Oxford) never affected consensual sex. I think I came across as rather highly strung and difficult in ordinary human intercourse, because I was shy, so men were often pleasantly surprised to find that in sexual intercourse I was quite different (my animal luck: my luck, again. Though of course it is also about both partners, and I can think of four or five times when I didn't enjoy it; once when the man was very much older, and something in me felt it was wrong, and shrivelled; twice when there had been a lot of begging and drinking but I still in my animal heart did not want it; once when the man in question and I had spun an overstretched myth of romance and the sex was doomed to be a disappointment, for my body was truthful when my mind was not.)

There followed more than a decade of practising before I found my lifetime partner. The sex, in itself, was enjoyable, and yet I never knew what lay behind it, and nor, I think, did my male partners. I was on the pill, so the obvious biological point of sex was missing, and besides, we were all deaf and blind to that aspect. I wasn't really pair-bonding. What was going on? I don't think we knew. The late sixties were an astonishing time. We were no longer using a rule-book. What did men want? What did women want?

What do women need? What do men need? I didn't have a clue in my twenties.

I don't have an answer even now. Except that the sexes intertwine. I have always felt both male and female, have always known I could be bisexual, though the love I cleaved to was heterosexual. Women need men; men, women. In my novel *The Ice People*, set forty years hence, in the middle of this century, I wrote about what I called 'segging', a segregation that comes upon the sexes as fertility drops and each gender turns inward, suspicious and hostile, resentful of what it is no longer being given. We aren't there yet, and I hope we never will be.

We need our own sex, especially as we grow up, to learn from, to relax with, to nurture and be nurtured; to form alliances that last a lifetime. (I went to a girls' grammar school, an all-female college.) But we also need our opposites. Gay men need mothers, grandmothers, aunts and female friends; lesbians need fathers, their own and their children's, grandfathers, uncles, male pals. Even hermits need someone to bring them food and drink, someone to admire their sacrifice.

I went through hermit phases in my twenties and very early thirties, trying to escape the messy relationships with men I had unconsciously pursued in the first place: not answering the doorbell, or the phone, or letters, not talking for days as I read or wrote. A reaction to sending too many letters, making unwise phone calls, seeing too many men, who sometimes turned up at the same time on my doorstep. I hadn't a clue how to deal with them. (Now I wouldn't touch men like those with a bargepole. What was I thinking? Alcoholics in the making, actors *manqués*, serial adulterers, glamorous but faintly sleazy men, the opposite of my upstanding father (which must have been the point. Of course it was the point.) Though most of them were also handsome and clever and fun, often from a higher social class than my own, ex-public school boys who knew restaurants and taxis. I was young, upwardly mobile, fond of sex. But why didn't I expect them to love and marry me? Was I trying to avoid a constricting marriage, or simply lacking in self-confidence? Trying to punish Vic, perhaps? Trying to prove I was as bad as he feared? Or avoiding the virginal path of my mother? I really don't know. A combination, surely.)

And I simplify, I simplify. We were all very young. Some of them were certainly fond, and romantic, and wrote me poems, but took their cue from me. One bought me my first adult perfume, in a pale coffee suede box: *Calèche,* by Hermès. He was poor, and a student, and it smelled of Paris, and I loved him for years, though we were wrong for each other. Some of them by now are reformed characters, kindly citizens, fathers, grandfathers (though some are dead, divorced, or drunks). We all got what we wanted, at least some of the time, and the rest of the time, we got what we deserved. But that sounds punitive. I don't want to punish my old raw self, so fresh from home, where nothing ever happened to prepare me for all this. I feel pity for that self, as well as shame. I had lived in a house where boundaries weren't respected, where the women placated an angry man. I tried too hard to please, at first. Slowly I learned to reassess what I deserved.

Something glorious I gained: a new name. The perfume-giver always called me Maggie. He knew actors; perhaps he was thinking of Maggie Smith. But almost as soon as I heard it, I liked it. I had always found my name burdensome. The 'Gee' was a problem, at Billingshurst Junior School, linking me to my head teacher father, making me mostly 'Gee-gee' (bearable) but sometimes the dreadful 'Dobbin's Daughter' – (unbearable, as I have said). 'Margaret' had come from Princess Margaret, but you needed the 'Princess' to carry it off. It had too many consonants, and wasn't beautiful, though I liked the meaning: pearl or daisy, as my mother told me when I asked her rather crossly why they'd called me that. But 'Margaret Gee' was all angles, assertive and solemn and rather smug, the name that was read out in school assemblies when I won a prize for something dull. When the chance arose, I couldn't wait to get rid of it. Maggie was my new self: racier, happier. Every time I hear it, it sounds affectionate. 'Maggie Gee' was an excellent name for a writer, three short, rhythmic feet, with that pleasing rhyme and definitive rhythm: *Magg-ie-GÈE, this-is-ME*. It was one of the best things those years yielded.

The late 1960s were not mono-gamous. I found it

Me being annoying at Oxford

all too possible to love two men at the same time. It is possible, but it never works out, is a recipe for excitement and confusion, followed by farce, conflict, sadness. One at a time is a very good rule, but of course it is the risk of conception that enforces it, and for the first time in the history of our species – think what that means: in the blink of an eye, they flower and die, a thousand generations of lovers – I and my friends did not fear it. In retrospect, though never at the time, I see that this changed everything. We were surfing the first wave of foolproof contraception, and the dark tide of AIDS was still far away, out in the ocean, unimaginable: neither death nor adulthood would ever come (they would, they did, but we were oblivious). We had few worries, we swam in the sunshine and played, and if it went wrong, moved on.

That was the theory, at any rate, though I often didn't want to move on when they did, or they didn't when I did, and it all went wrong; suddenly we were back on dry land; scenes on stairs, or outside stations. These often seemed to involve transport, which was fitting, given the men's fleet-footedness. I remember one scene (though not the narrative context) when one gloriously dashing and polygamous swain, made voluble and highly persuasive by whisky but also insane and uncoordinated, was trying to persuade me we should leave an Intercity train, by the door, as we sped through the Oxfordshire countryside. I stopped him; at a deep level, despite my superficially risky behaviour, I always wanted to survive, and I did. Only once did I get to the point of asking for tranquillisers when something went wrong, for I have always been shy of medication, have never even taken a sleeping pill, though I go through phases of not sleeping. I remember sobbing on the floor at home, with the Valium pills in their packaging inside a paper bag three feet away on the table. *I would go to the table, pick up the bag, open the packaging, take the pill.* And the nearness of the possibility was so shocking that I stopped crying and got up off the floor. At some level I still loved my consciousness, even though it was a consciousness of pain and folly, and feared changing it, and losing myself.

I remember sex in a churchyard; in a garden; in a room at a party where no one else was; with a famous male-to-female transexual and his friend (not half-way concluded, for obvious reasons). And yet I daresay I was having less sex than people who had quietly married at twenty. But the rest of the time I read and wrote, and I never did anyone's washing or cooking, which left me much time to get on with my writing, which I did in a solid and serious way, and I did not even think about babies. I was learning, very slowly, more about men, and something about what it meant to be a woman.

My best relationships then were with girls. My friend Barbara Goodwin, for example, a funny, brilliant, reed-thin redhead who knew more about everything than me, and taught me I could go to art galleries and theatres, and drove us to Yugoslavia, where I cooked hideous fry-ups of mackerel and we looked at huge stars over the unlit sea, and talked about Gilbert Ryle's philosophy, and slowly revealed to each other the truth about our childhoods, as growing distance allowed us to discern it.

At first I read her comically wrong. She was a Somerville Scholar, like me, and with the tact of Oxford education at the time, we not only had different gowns from the 'commoners', we were also housed separately in swanky new rooms. (*Commoners*! The tactlessness was unbelievable. Well done, Oxford! At the time, though, I was thankful to be a little queen. I came from Billingshurst, I had to have something.) But Barbara had a room further up the corridor, and came in and out quite late at night. She was beautiful, with her pale heart-shaped face and thick red hair waving over her shoulders, and dressed exquisitely in 1960s fashion, velvet and ruffles, long boots and long earrings, a floor-length patchwork coat, beady-eyed fox furs. When she spoke, her voice was thrillingly aristocratic, with glowing oval vowels like small stained glass windows. I was in love with her; I longed for her to be my friend, but wouldn't that

Barbara in Paris in 1982

always be impossible? She swept about alone and dated young dons. At the beginning of the second term, she was coming upstairs as I was going down. A small smiling man, balding and cheery, was carrying up her cases. I thought, *I suppose it is her butler.* I tolerated this amiable representative of the working classes but I wanted him to leave me alone with Barbara. Only after he was gone did I learn, amazed, that this man was in fact Tom Goodwin, her father, that the peerless Barbara was from my own class, was naturally stylish, and had taken elocution. We were class congruous. I need not be afraid! Our friendship came on by leaps and bounds. She drove down to Billingshurst; she met my father. *She knew all about me and still liked me.* She would be my friend for the rest of my life.

In 1985 – I was married, she wasn't – we went on holiday *à deux* to a lovely old Victorian hotel in Swanage, and on a whim, visited a fortune-teller, Katina, who had a booth on Swanage pier. I have visited more than one fortune-teller, but Katina was in a class of her own. She was young, and though she said she was a gypsy, had no robes or earrings, no affectation or spookiness or mystery. She grasped my hand, looked into my eyes, and then spoke brightly, specifically, swiftly, without hesitation, in a down-to-earth voice that told me many things: my husband would work for the BBC (he had shown no signs of it, but she was right); our house would get subsidence; I would care for my mother. In retrospect I wish I had taken up the offer to tape her predictions, as Barbara did. Almost everything Katina told us came to pass. For Barbara she saw, and described with eerie accuracy, the husband she would meet two years later, a much older man in a powerful position, witty, erudite Michael Miller, QC, who would adore her, as Katina promised, and was married to her until his death last year. I enjoyed writing it on envelopes: 'Professor Barbara Goodwin and Mr Michael Miller, QC,' because part of me could never quite believe that life would bring such substance to the girls we had been; that we would end up with serious men, good men who wanted to marry us.

My precious cast of women friends, most of them made during those vital years for same-sex friendships, that time between leaving home and pair-bonding. Hilary Soper, my girlfriend from the age of eleven at grammar school, an identical twin of five foot ten; an accident of geography meant we lived only a few miles apart from seventeen to twenty-one. Hilary, with whom I've never had a cross word in nearly fifty years of friendship; who makes sure a sprinkling of cakes and jokes, postcards, small treats and kindnesses, are there to sweeten life's lemon-peel spiral. When I think of Hilary, I see us wandering down a succession of long light rooms in the galleries where we often meet, looking at pictures as we tell our stories in a relaxed, amicable rhythm, for we have known for decades that we have our whole lives to explain ourselves; but when friends tell all, there are sadnesses, and our eyes meet, we feel it together, we want nothing bad to happen to each other, but we know the gallery stretches on past, we cast about for another picture, some sunlit Dufy or golden Bonnard. When we were girls, we seemed to have nothing, and the whole mountain range was ahead of us. Somehow, by the miracle of days becoming years, Hilary became a head teacher, raised a kind son, Luke, on her own, and now lives with an art expert, her gentle, handsome husband Alistair, in an old Sussex cottage full of books and pictures. How did it happen? How do things work out? How do men and women ever find one another?

Women friends, though, came easily. First Elan, Joy, Lydia, who lived with cats and dogs and rabbits and sewed the wing back on to a goose, and could have run a bank or a global company, then Pippa, Lesley, and shortly after, Grania, Nina and Rachel, Fatima, Carolyn; then Caroline, Hanna, Penny, Bernardine; most recently, vivid Ana, the dancer. So many kind and clever women. They are mostly still here: our story goes on.

Two other women's names from my rackety twenties make me pause longer and look away. Tiny Australian Beverly Hayne, my friend when I finally staggered to London, delivered by Pippa in a rented van. Bev was a journalist for glossy magazines, with short red-gold hair, fine skin, a small bird-nose and neat little bird-feet, a husky voice, a breathless laugh – perhaps too breathless? She found me a job as a hotel receptionist, since I was sick of doing degrees, and paid for my first publishing party (and made so light of it I hardly noticed, but now I am amazed; so much kindness, though she also tended to quick bouts of annoyance: 'Doncha just hate it when …?') – the funniest, perhaps, of so many funny women, passionate, short-tempered, creative, inventive. She was irritated by my messes and excesses, but she thought I had talent, believed in me, and wrote a spoof autobiography for me, decades before this one, longhand, for my birthday, 'My Life' by Maggie Gee, complete with witty drawings to which she attached scraps of coloured satin, sequins, a feather, and bound it in cardboard sheathed in black silk. She had the drive and wit to become famous as a writer – but her Australian family were too poor and too rural to fix a faulty heart-valve when she was young, so the doctors forbade her to risk having children with sweet-tempered Andy whom she married in London, and though she had escaped from poverty, though her pluck and will-power took her halfway round the world, she died, one morning, getting up too quickly when her loving husband was away on a trip, in their chic modern flat, of a heart attack. She was in her mid-thirties, painfully young.

We had booked the first holiday of our married lives, but the dates clashed with the funeral. Andy said 'Go'. Guiltily, we went to Portugal; I knew I shouldn't, but oh, I wanted to, and we had little money, so the air fare we had already paid seemed enormous. I wrote a poem to be read at the service. I should have been there, to speak up for my friend, but Andy and destiny sent me somewhere different. On that holiday, in that fierce spring light, urged on by death, which made the shadows sharper, far away from rational considerations (we had nowhere to live, no security, but I was thirty-seven, time rushed onwards), I became pregnant with my daughter. It would never have happened if we'd stayed at home. You could see it as the final gift from Beverly's friendship.

Girls, my girls, *mes soeurs*, my sisters.

Then there's Kitty Mrosovsky, the aristocratic, literary beauty whose Russian father was a friend of Nabokov's, president of Somerville JCR when I first saw her, hurrying gracefully against the daylight, in a narrow-waisted coat, her long dark hair pulled casually up under a Russian fur hat, calling to some out-of-focus girls in her wake. I never thought she would become my friend, yet she liked me, and invited me, later, to her tiny icy house near Arsenal, full of books and pictures and elegant poverty, because she had, I think, a minute private income which encouraged her to give up a prestigious university job and wager everything on being a writer. Perhaps all her life she gave up too much. She completed the definitive translation of Flaubert's *Temptation of St Anthony*, with notes: but it was the study of a hermit. She wrote difficult novels, played piano sonatas, and banished grief with hot baths and yoga, and I was a little in awe of her, though she welcomed me, and was amusedly fond of the chaotic, excitable child I was. Like many of these friends, she mothered me, perhaps sensing there were things my own mother couldn't give me; but she died of AIDS, too early to be wary, infected by a brilliant American boyfriend who was bisexual before anyone knew the dangers. He was African American, he taught at Yale, he was handsome and muscular and full of life. He wanted to marry her, but she refused. She was obstinate, reserved, fastidious, tender. She grew thinner, and withdrew from her friends, not wanting to bother them, not wanting to be ill, still hurrying down the street, still light-boned and graceful, and then too light, and suddenly gone. Her fate seemed bizarre, impossible. Her voice was beautiful; a light silver singsong. She had two sisters who adored her. That dangerous freedom. Death crept in from the horizon. We thought we knew everything; we didn't see the future. We needed men, but men could destroy us.

Dear girls of my youth. What talk, what laughter! Only death has parted us. We shared so much as we struggled to be adults; ordinary cheerfulness, everyday intimacy, luck, disaster; we cared for each other. Talking about men, sharing knowledge, telling stories against ourselves, helping each other to find our way in a world where marriage was no longer obvious. In those days, I was married to my female friends. Yet I needed those badly-judged relationships with men. How else could I have made the transition from the oppressions of home to my own, freeer marriage? If you behave for too long, in the end you break out. I carried a burden of anger and sorrow, sorrow for my mother, anger with my father, though I should have felt sorrow for him as well, and I do, now he no longer weighs on me. He didn't teach me what was tolerable, how much or how little I should yield to men. I found that out, through a decade of conflict. I slowly worked towards a way of being happy.

And now I am no longer young (though I feel it), so if I am to answer this chapter's questions, it had better be now, before I start forgetting the scraps of knowledge life has left on my sleeve. I grew up with men. I always knew them. But I learned more slowly how to deal with them.

I like men, as friends, as colleagues, as fathers – it moves me to see men with their children, especially since I have entered the world of parents and children – as sexual partners and objects of desire. I love young men for their maleness, their angles, their shiny skins and their firm jaws, their hopefulness and brashness, their risk-taking, their certainty, their shyness mixed with confidence, their courage and light-heartedness. I like the clear line of their necks and shoulders, the bone and muscle jutting bravely at the sky. I'm not sexually attracted to young men; what would I do with one, if I got him? I wouldn't enjoy feeling elderly stretched out alongside some dazzling Apollo. But I would have loved to have a son, as well as a daughter. I would have loved to give Nick a son.

From my family of men, of brothers and fathers and uncles and boy cousins, I learned to love men, and to see them as touching, though I also learned they were explosive and needy. *I mustn't give everything. Stand my ground.* Yet sexually, I yielded too easily. I wanted to please them, as well as myself. I wanted to please them, or I wanted to placate them?

What do men need from women? The answers I grope for don't come from having got this right, but from getting it wrong, and seeing others get it wrong.

I think they want appreciation of their male virtues. There are lovable traits which I do see as male, not that they are exclusively so. Being brave or rash or funny, devoting themselves to single tasks or causes. Being physically strong. Having big ideas. Dreaming, carrying, and making. Founding states or cities, being ready to die for them. Forgiveness for their male faults: being one-track minded, forgetting the details, not noticing what's going on emotionally, disliking being told about it, not wanting to talk (though sometimes that's a virtue), thinking they are sick when they are not, being too ready to fight and die or send others off to do so for a cause. (Of course many women also do these things.)

But what if men use their strength the wrong way? What if they prevail by violence, or fear? Then they need a woman to stand up to them, or leave them. A sad fact: most of us behave as badly as the people who live with us allow.

I have seen how men like to have motherly care. Acceptance, rather than amused, sneering toleration, of their masculine bodies. Sex as an expression of that absolute acceptance and tenderness, which often means oral sex. Men want to be wanted, just like women. Some have been amazed when I wanted them. Emotional closeness – when they feel like it. Friendship. To be listened to. To be admired for the efforts they make, and respected.

Not to be belittled, in public or private. A home where the father is truly welcome, not excluded, plotted against, marginalised. Children who are encouraged by the mother to love them. It sounds obvious, but it doesn't always happen. This was the guerrilla war my mother fought, because she didn't dare do anything braver. So she kept Dad in the dark, and laughed at him. Not always, though: 'Your dad's a good provider.' And 'Don't upset Dad.' But also 'Don't tell Dad.' So the kitchen would fall silent when Dad came in. It wasn't a good feeling. It didn't make him happy.

What do women need from men? What do I need to be happy? Many of the same things, of course. Love, tenderness, not to be belittled (though I like to be teased. It's a conundrum.) A child, friendly companionship, a home.

I know my mother craved recognition for the care she gave to men and to children, to Dad and to Grandpa, after his stroke, to all of us: she cooked every single meal, shopped and planned, paid bills and made appointments, did the washing and ironing. To be fair, my father often said thank you, and so does my husband, which is very important, though he has much less to thank me for, because nobody irons, and there's a washing machine.

Sometimes women need care from men in return. There my own father did less well. When Mum was ill for a month after giving birth to my younger brother, he cooked soft-boiled eggs at furious speed: shuddering whites, still transparent, with the coiling cord fully visible, and would not learn, though no one could eat them, and the eggs ended up on the side of the plate, small crumbled abortions, viscous and gleaming, stuck over with messy mosaics of shell: alternating this treat with 'Vermicelli Cheese', his favourite dish, which he cooked quite well, but its regular wormy gleam made us hate it. Whereas my husband cooks fluently and cheerfully, modern, interesting food with lots of ginger and garlic, chopping vegetables with the radio on, not fussing, asking only to be left alone; and always brings me cups of tea in the morning, when I am obtuse and drugged with sleep, having fizzed and gabbled in the early hours while he is dropping off like a baby.

I like appreciation of my female virtues: making things beautiful, seeing to the details. Mostly it's women who do the flowers, tracking them down in the winter garden, the last peaky rose, a red geranium leaf, a Japanese lantern minus half its blazing orange but revealing the elaborate lace of its structure; together on the table, they're a small miracle. Lovely when a man enjoys it. My green-fingered mother expressed herself by growing African violets from seed, and had Africa in bloom in every corner of her bleak '60s kitchen, white, pink, mauve, lush and plump-leaved, insubordinate, and another year, the toothed hearts of coleus, flame shooting out of the pink Formica.

Is it mostly women who notice when people are unhappy? Maybe. Maybe we're more porous to other people. That gives us a chance to offer comfort. (But sometimes it's better to glide over things; if you see what's going on, it becomes harder for the sufferer to choose to hide it; and men know that instinctively.)

We show realism when dealing with dreams, though this can also be the vice of small-mindedness. And women are funny in a different way; we enjoy telling stories against ourselves. We find ourselves ridiculous.

We endure hardships, and remember dull things – dates, schedules, responsibilities. But no one is ever going to thank us for this, particularly when the tasks are to be done by others. 'Have you written that thank you letter to your sister? Did you remember your maths homework?' I am sometimes the Lexicon of Other People's Duties. Nobody likes a lexicon.

We need forgiveness for our female faults: obsessing about detail, worrying too much, talking about feelings when men don't want to, criticising, thinking about the past, cleaning up when we could be having fun. Guilty on all counts, your honour. (But of course men do all these things too.)

We need to be seen as individuals, people who exist outside the home. I have always taken this for granted; I shouldn't. My father didn't want my mother to work.

Loyalty as we age from a good lover, who goes on wanting and desiring us. To be made to feel beautiful, however old we are.

If many of these primal needs aren't met, love turns to enmity, tenderness to meanness, the couple shrinks in lemon juice.

Living through time in a couple isn't easy. Lives have become very long. Deep and friendly love between a man and a woman is not the easiest thing to find. I can think of a bare dozen happy couples among the many I have known.

But then, it's 2009, as I write. These are still trying, transitional times. Only in 1919 did British women get the vote. Ninety years ago: that means women are alive who remember their own mothers being unable to vote. Is the problem that we still haven't got over the war? It is very recent, the period when women were not allowed to graduate, nor to have a claim on their children when marriages broke down. It amazes today's confident young women to hear that, less than a lifetime ago, women were allowed, as a concession, to go to university, but were not allowed to take degrees. The rage and scorn women show to men – the contempt of female columnists, the boring venting against 'hopeless Harry' – might just be an unconscious mirror image of the scorn men formerly showed women, when they forbade them half of life.

All the same, scorn helps no one. If you want to get the best from someone, you have to be ready to see something good in them.

(Easy enough to say, but I wish I was always kind, and loving. I know that I am not. I can be cutting, irascible, unfair. The war is in me, and in all of us. We fight for recognition, for freedom from the boredom of small duties – who does what? – for respect of our needs, for space, for money. We fight to be equal, though we know we're not the same. There are no servants any more to liberate middle-class women from household drudgery; and in any case, when servants were the rule, my family were the servants, I would have been a servant, as my maternal grandmother was. I am still fighting not to be downtrodden like my mother, though no one has ever trodden me down, in fact. Because of my father, I can't bear my husband shouting, and yet I sometimes shout at him. He has never hit me. If he did, I would leave him.)

As I write that, I see it's just showing off. I would assume he had gone mad, and find a way of forgiving him. There is so much love and friendship between us. So many years I can't live again with someone else. And there's our daughter: in her our love goes on into the future.

But what if I'd never met Nick? What then? I was awkward, and damaged, and weird enough not to have lived with anyone. Not to have had a child. I feel I would have missed the point.

Then the gift of Nick's unconditional love changed everything for me. A man loved me completely, and I became a woman. In a world of two, and then three, I could grow.

He needed me. I needed him.

11 My animal luck (v)

my advice:
very unwise to give it

As the reader may have noticed, life tends to rush upon me, new and shining, out of the blue, and I am dazzled, and only grasp the meaning of it decades later, as I relive the days. The good things that befall me seem to come by luck and, more especially, the kindness of others. I have realised it more as I write this memoir: how very little we can do alone.

I met Nick in early spring 1981, in a pub-theatre, the York and Albany, an isolated building at the end of one arm of Camden Town, squeezed between roaring roads and the horse chestnut buds of Regent's Park. It was all thanks to my friend Kitty Mrosovsky, who invited me to a performance of a play by 'Mouth and Trousers'. She was writing theatre reviews for a journal called *Quarto*, and her last piece had been about a play called *Arrest*: Nick's first play, whose run had just finished.

By chance, the young playwright was there that night. He was thin and intense, with fine Celtic features, strong jaw and expressive eyebrows, blue-grey eyes, narrow well-shaped nose. Tall, handsome, dark, serious; simple traits I attached to him. Of course, he wanted to impress us. This was the first time he had met Kitty, and she had admired his work in print. I thought theirs would be a match made in heaven, and found something to do so they could talk on their own. They were both in the same idiom, somehow, though he was in jeans and navy pea-coat, and she in something relaxed and classic (whereas, I, as usual, was dressed like a vamp, in a black zipped jumpsuit, diamante drop earrings, and an old black fur with a shot-silk lining, pink lipstick and long blonde hair). Perhaps I picked up something else as well, for though no one mentioned it, they'd both gone to public school – that mad English usage where public means private. Shrewsbury was talking to Benenden. And Horsham High School made herself scarce.

Nick, in 1970, aged twenty, when he lived just across the road from me in Oxford – had we met then, it would never have worked

But at the end of the evening, he had both our phone numbers. Chance: pure chance that I met my beloved, and that I met him then – when the timing was perfect; he was at the end of a long relationship. He was thirty, and I was thirty-two. We were friends for eighteen months before we started dating.

I showed zero perspicacity about the future, because I brought sense and logic to bear, whereas Nick knew we were right together by physical instinct. I told my friend Barbara, 'He's very attractive, I fancy him madly, but I know I could never fall in love with him. He talks all the time. He's not my type.'

Whereas the very first time Nick was alone with me, not many weeks after we met in the theatre, he walked me to the local pub, sat me down, and said, about ten minutes into the conversation, 'I'm going to take you to America. In fact, I think we should get married.' Even he looked surprised as soon as he had said it. As he told me much later, he had never said anything like that before, to anyone, but something came over him, or spoke through him. I laughed and ignored it, thinking, 'He's mad,' little knowing that just over two years later I would stand by his side, trembling but happy, in a white Victorian satin nightdress, as we said our vows in a Cambridge registry office.

I didn't have a clue about any of it. Yet still I am tempted to give advice. Still I believe I'm a bit of an expert.

Viewed benignly, advice is just sharing tips, a habit of female gleaners and gatherers. While male hunters silently stalk their prey, not deigning to ask which way is north, the women back at camp are telling each other which herbs best flavour the flesh of mammoth.

How I thirst to pass on knowledge. My last chapter, about men and women, was stiff with advice, stuffed with it. I persevere despite the boredom of my listener. I must simply advise with more pep and vim! I must improve the lives of others! I crash boldly onwards through their thickets of unease. A good spot for a holiday, a dental insurance plan, the perils of putting lemons in the compost ...

I hand out my tips like elaborate, generous gifts from one life to another. But by middle age, people don't want gifts. Their houses are already loaded with stuff, they know about holidays, teeth, and lemons (pancakes with lemon and sugar. My tip is, avoid them: a double hex on your dentine.)

In my family – meaning me, Nick, my daughter – the most annoying advice is given when someone has just started on the recommended course of action. 'Why don't you dry the glasses/put your shoes on/ bring a coat?' 'I'm doing it, *I'm doing it*!' the wretched advisee cries.

Of course, sometimes people ask for advice. That's when it's important to hold back, because they are vulnerable, and may take it. But can I hold back? It is *so* tempting.

So flattering when someone consults you. The belief that life's actually taught you something. Suddenly you feel useful, which doesn't often happen to a writer. Yet other people's lives are just that, other. Most useless of all to advise on people's lovers. Of course Y is trouble, or Z is appalling, but don't advise Y to give Z up. They will get married, and never call you.

The problem is, I myself long for advice. I seek it, eagerly, from everyone. I want to learn lessons from other people's lives. It's part of my essential optimism. I really believe I can make most things better, if only I can find out enough about them. When pregnant, I brooded over pregnancy books; as a young mother, baby books; though adolescence books always seemed a pale shadow of the storm and glory we were going through. I read all the health pages in newspapers; I study *New Scientist* for new 'work' on anything touching the human condition which I can pass on to my husband or daughter (she defends herself with ribald humour. 'Oh God, Mum, don't tell me you've found more "work". My mother thinks there is *work* on everything,' Rosa tells her friends, when I try to educate them on, say, the effects of black chocolate on cholesterol. '*Work! Work!*,' she shrieks, and she is laughing so much she chokes on her milk chocolate).

But her grandmother, like me, was a fund of useful tips. 'Never leave washing-up until the morning,' Mum said (and 'Red sky at night, shepherd's delight. Red sky in the morning, shepherd's warning.') And 'This won't buy the baby a new bonnet.' 'Always do the bed, it makes the room look tidy.' 'Don't forget to tie a knot in your cotton.' 'Tie a knot in your hanky to remember something.' 'Don't trust people who show the whites of their eyes under the iris.' (Did this mean my mother distrusted the blind?) 'You don't want to be mutton dressed up as lamb.' 'Don't drink from the bottle, it looks bad.' (She had a point, since we were driving through respectable streets, it was before midday, and I was swigging British sherry, but she was leaving my father, temporarily, and the pressure was getting to me.)

'Come to the breast-screening van!' she bade me. 'I take any screening I can get. It's all on the NHS, it's great!' It was a common feeling among the generation who saw the Health Service's miraculous beginnings. I went with Mum, in my mid-twenties, to the breast-screening van in the windy gravel car-park. There my breasts were compressed between two hard metal plates, which were squeezed together till I felt like screaming. Later I discovered that in women under fifty the risk of having cancer is outweighed by the chance of cancer started by the X-ray.

Never give advice. No one will thank you.

And yet, in my sex life, and my love life, I needed advice, and my mother couldn't give it. This is no criticism; she was unequipped. She only ever slept with one man, my father, and she felt completely at sea in the sixties. (Just as the young were; we were making it up. We felt we were free in an enormous playground, and when we spotted people crying in the corners, it seemed like an error on their part; and when *we* were the hurt ones, we felt at fault, for the new rules, surely, should benefit us all.)

Why, then, did some of us have bad dreams?

Mum's dissatisfaction with her own marriage meant she did not want to foist the same thing on her daughter. Instead she struggled to understand the tortuous comings and goings in my emotional life. It couldn't be good that I was having a relationship with a married man, could it? Or with more than one man at once? And yet she was reluctant to judge. If he loved me, this might be better than the narrow logic of her own life. Did it make me happy? she asked. I gave her some simplified version of the truth. She only wanted me to be happy, she said. If I loved X, she would too. She never asked me – as my teens sprinted into my twenties, then my late twenties, and I lived on my own; turned thirty, thirty-one, thirty-two – whether I wanted to get married, or have children. And to give him his due, nor did my father. Once I was an adult, they left me alone to make my own mistakes, which I did.

But now I see we did need some advice, we liberated women, from the elders of the tribe. I was living my life in a piecemeal way, as an individualist, a thinker, a writer. I lived in my head, and had sex with my body, and my heart beat fast when I listened to music, the glorious music of love of the sixties, Motown, the Beatles, the Stones, Soul, the sublime hanging gardens of 'A Whiter Shade of Pale'. My heart seemed to recognise a longing for love that was not fulfilled by the life I led, but my head came to no conclusions, and my body continued to enjoy itself. The three of us hardly spoke to each other.

Yet my unconscious was semaphoring frantically to me. I began to have dreams, one of the only two recurring dreams of my life, in which I'd had a tiny baby, but lost it. It had fallen on the floor, or rolled under a chair, and I'd forgotten about it, not fed it, lost it. Sometimes there was more than one midget baby. This dream came again and again, insistent, a few months apart, until it was familiar, and so was the feeling of sadness it brought, the attempt, too late, to find the missing dream-infant, from which I always awoke empty-handed. One day I told this dream to my friend Barbara, who was also on the pill, like me, and having sex, but not getting pregnant. Although she had never wanted children, she told me that she had the same dreams. The fine hair on my arms stood on end. And then we both asked other young women. Many of us turned out to share the same dream life.

We were all guinea-pigs in a chemical war that was being waged in the recesses of our bodies. Of course we didn't consciously see what we were doing, we clever undergraduates, we liberated women, but the collective unconscious was savvier than us. Our bodies had found a way of talking to us, showing the ghost babies that weren't being born, for the pill did not always prevent conception; it also stopped fertilised eggs implanting. We were watching our own dramas while we slept, but our waking selves remained strangely unmoved.

Of course my parents were not able to advise me. What was happening was so utterly different from the world they had known, the war, rationing, the hasty marriages to keep women safe and allow the men to have babies before they faced death. They had been short of everything, including sexual information, in the nineteen-thirties, when they were young. Both of them were virgins in 1944, when they married each other, my father aged thirty, my mother twenty-seven. My mother was pregnant with my brother that year and still thought that babies came out of the belly, which would part down the line from navel to pubis. Her mother had told her absolutely nothing. And then when the straitlaced, family fifties replaced the frenzy of the war, sexual freedom was in short supply. They had too little, and we too much.

Now I look at my daughter's generation, and things have changed again, but I suspect there is more in common between my nineteen-sixties and Rosa's two-thousands than there was between my generation and my mother's. I talk to my daughter. We talk to each other. I can at least tell her the mistakes I made, though she, of course, will learn from her own, a better way of learning than by hearing advice.

Better but more painful. I learned through sorrow. Pleasure in the short run, tears later. This is what I learned. If you want to have children, choose a marrying man, and the choice of those is wider when you are younger. A marrying man, not a married man. There are men who want to marry and have children, but they tend to get snapped up before the others. By twenty-five, a lot of them have already gone. Around thirty, the last proto-dads are homing keenly in on the proto-mums. If a woman doesn't start searching till she's in her thirties, the odds are less good, and the search more desperate.

It's crude, it's glib, but it's roughly true. I do believe we learn from other people's experience; it must be one reason why language skills evolved.

(Only two of my close friends began their families in their twenties. Most of us girls never gave it a thought. One of those two was Pippa, a doctor's daughter. 'My father always told us, have your first child before you're thirty.' This piece of advice from an elder bore fruit. Uniquely among my clutch of graduate friends, Pippa has three grown up children.)

Mum gave no advice about marriage or children, but her folk wisdom came into play when I told her that Nick and I, who had been dating for four months or so, were helping my friend Barbara to refurbish her Holland Park flat. We were spending days happily artexing ceilings and painting walls together, side by side. 'Nest-building,' Mum said. 'You're nest-building.'

Before long we came to stay with Mum and Dad for the weekend. Nick had borrowed a little yellow Beetle car from his friend John. My parents were welcoming – no wonder: I hadn't brought many boys to meet them. I didn't trust the boys to like them: nor was I sure they would agree to come. My mother was captivated when we went for a walk and Nick worried in case I would be cold, and made me put a jacket on. I wasn't so sure about Dad's reaction; Nick had admitted he didn't like football. My father loved football. All men should like football.

Things took a major turn for the worse next morning when Nick and I set off for the sea. On our speedy way out Nick barged the yellow VW into our neighbour's low chain fence, flattening a post or two. 'Oh god oh god,' I said, but Nick was already driving off, at high speed, had gone, by now, too far to turn back, leaving the evidence of our guilt behind us. I was shocked, but giggling with panic and excitement. Nick has always had an antic self, a self of rash or dashing acts and surreal invented voices, *improvistos*. And yet, on the small white beach at Weybourne, his arm sheltering me from the breeze, we had a short talk and agreed we would get married, and when we went home, he asked my father.

They had been amused, thank God, by the fence, which could only mean one thing: they really liked him. My father was capable of turning that into a crime, but instead he had seen himself in Nick's shoes; it was the act of a nervous, eager suitor. 'Vic, I would like to marry your daughter.' My father laughed soundlessly and tossed back his head in the way he did when he was happy, but he guarded himself against sentiment. 'I expect you will whatever I say,' he riposted, robustly, but he shook Nick's hand. Nick would do for his unmarried daughter.

He did more than 'do'. They both came to adore him. My mother loved his good looks and charm, and of course, the way he did not bully me. She did not worry that he was poor; she was right, he became a good, steady earner, though we Rankin-Gees have never been rich. They both loved his humour, especially the absurd characters he suddenly improvised from nowhere, a heritage from his ancestry – Sarah Siddons, the famous eighteenth-century actress, was his great-great-great-great-great-grandmother – which sent them into paroxysms of laughter. Later, when he became a BBC broadcaster, they listened loyally to his programmes, bent over the radio in the kitchen, though World Service reception was bad in Norfolk, and wrote him long appreciative letters.

'I love young men,' Mum said to me, in much the same words that I use now. 'There's something lovely about young men.' He was there when she was dying, only nine years later, making her laugh in the hospital on the very last evening of her life with a joke that plays upon a less romantic side of tenderness across the generations. It has to be said with a strong Norfolk burr:

'Arrr yew goin' ter com up Weely Woods with me tonoight, gurl?'

'No-ow! Moy mothuhr wooden' loik it.'

'*Yowur mothuhr ain' goin' ter geddit!*'

('Are you going to come up Weely Woods with me tonight, girl?'

'No! My mother wouldn't like it.'

'Your mother ain't going to get it!')

Many people would be doubtful about deathbed jokes, but it was exactly the right thing for Mum. Nick knew that, as he knows so many things, whereas I waste hours debating and doubting. It must be why, when he wants to sleep, his breathing changes and he's gone within seconds.

Mostly it's the really big things he gets right. In 1986, he had just finished his first book, *Dead Man's Chest: Travels after Robert Louis Stevenson*. Nick had delivered to Faber, but got no word. Then Beverly died, and though I agonised, we did as Andy kindly urged us, and went on the holiday we had planned. It had a special significance: we were meeting my parents there, to celebrate Dad's birthday, in the Algarve that they loved, where they spent every winter, the treat that, mysteriously, saved them money. I had never been to Portugal. We had our flights booked, and a double room at a strange hotel I must have found in a brochure.

It sat on a strip of Algarve coast which was in the throes of savage butchery as huge roads and sewers and foundations for skyscrapers were forced into the earth, which lay spreadeagled, wounded. We tried to walk at night, and parts of the town were like another planet, grassless and treeless, inhabited by big silent machines.

Our own hotel had been dropped here, at random, from somewhere in Scandinavia. It was white, vast, almost uninhabited, like an uglier version of the Snow Queen's palace, blank, pointless atrium after atrium, with silent rooms to either side. Everything was new: the grass had not grown. There were water-features everywhere. Perhaps that was why the whole wintry fantasy smelled overwhelmingly of pine disinfectant, a terrible, sharp, chemical greenness inimical to anything growing.

We managed to bear it for two days or so, and strode down the coast a mere half-hour's walk to have a memorably happy, vinous lunch with my parents in a local restaurant whose owner they loved. They were so proud to introduce us to Alfonso: *our daughter the writer* and her handsome husband. *Yes, he is a writer too!* The pride was two-way; I was touched and surprised to see the owner knew them and seemed fond of them, as if they ate out often, and were accepted. All through my childhood, 'going out' had been dangerous, and my nerves had been jangling, that morning, as we walked by the sea, but age had smoothed enough of Dad's combativeness away for them to be happy, and us to be happy. For a few golden hours, we sat and enjoyed the new symmetry that came from my marriage and the mysterious specialness that family acquired by being hundreds of miles away from home, in a strange bare landscape where all else was new. What were these tendrils of connectedness, this sudden warm familiarity that clung around us in a world inhuman as the moon? What did family mean? Something new was stirring.

Afterwards I remember standing in the blaze of heat by the wayside, waiting for my parents' taxi to come. It took half an hour longer than expected. They looked small and old in the ferocious light. Once they would not have needed a taxi. But Nick was in high good humour, and for some reason he began to impersonate a Teddy Boy going out on a Friday night, walking down the road with chest absurdly inflated, ape arms swinging, knees doing a springy dance of self-importance. Instead of worrying about the taxi, my parents laughed and laughed, especially my father, who shook and wept, yielding to the moment, free of all anxiety, shoulders soundlessly heaving, pale eyes streaming in the sunlight. Nick marched up and down: we couldn't stop laughing. 'He's very funny, duck,' Dad said as we parted. 'He's a real comedian, is Nick.' It was high praise, the gift of a tribute.

I think perhaps that lunch was important. It was all leading somewhere, but I didn't know where. I did know we couldn't stay a moment longer in the ice-white Viking monstrosity I'd chosen. Despite the glassy-eyed despair of the staff, who sat there paralysed, with nothing to do, servicing international emptiness, we checked out, and walked towards the sea, and found ourselves something more ordinary, cheaper. It had coaches outside, but at least there were people. The breakfast was economy class, with orange squash and white rolls and jam, but what mattered was the room. And what happened inside it.

At first they showed us to a room with single beds. 'No,' I said, and they swiftly moved us. The next room, at first, seemed equally bad, though at least it had a double bed. But it looked over a blank field of rubble. 'What's this?' I asked the man who had brought us here. 'Ees a factory,' he said. 'But they knock heem down.' He made it sound as if this was a bonus.

'I don't want a view of a demolished factory!' I said to Nick, who was staring out of the window. He didn't want to move again.

'OK,' I sighed, and the man left us.

'Look,' said Nick. 'Look again.'

Some obelisk or pole had been left standing out there, alone in the middle of a muddle of rubbish.

No, it wasn't a pole, it was a chimney.

With something large and black on top.

As I watched, I saw something was moving in that dark disk, small flickering changes to the sharp silhouette. And then a huge bird swooped down from the blue, with wide white wings, elaborate, angelic, catching the sunlight, transforming the view.

'It's a stork,' I said. 'Of course, it's a stork's nest.'

'Yes,' said Nick, 'and there are young.'

We watched them whenever we were in the room. We made jokes, of course, about the storks bringing babies. The rest of the time, we discovered how much of the Lagos peninsula was still unspoiled, if you got away from the mangled centre. We walked for hours along tiny goat-tracks; goats fled ahead of us, a flash of light coats, bells clanging erratic, melancholy notes; the herbs on the slopes down to the sea were aromatic; there were lemon-trees and mimosa trees and tiny spring flowers – rock roses, tiny golden pea-flowers, miniature indigo irises, dark tongues in mouths of speckled flame. The light made everything unnaturally clear, as if we were being shown something, as if God had pulled a grey curtain away, and here it was, dazzling and complex, his handiwork. There was something almost brutal about so much beauty that we in our studies did not usually see. At night we walked along deserted beaches. They were not romantic; they made me shiver. The waves crashed hard upon great black rocks that blazed red by daylight. The moon was full, unbelievably large, and stared at us, hard, effortlessly burning our eyes with silver. I thought about Beverly, whose life was over. Nick, who had just given up smoking, was in an uncharacteristic mood, his system disrupted by the lack of nicotine, and feeling wild and rootless now his book was finished and he had nothing definite lined up.

I was ready with good advice, as usual. 'You need a niche somewhere,' I said. 'Something that isn't me, or writing. I think that men need somewhere to go.' I must have based that idea on my father, who set off every morning at half-past eight. I wasn't entirely wrong, as it happened, but in another sense I was completely blind, for there was something else that we both needed, which stared us in the face, and only I couldn't see it, something that was happening all around us in the dazzling display of plants and animals.

Ever since we had been a couple, we had used contraception, but Nick had long ago suggested I come off the pill, and he was right, for I had been on it for a decade. We had never taken risks; I'm a cautious person, who likes to make logical decisions. I had told him when we married that I didn't want children, because I thought they would stop me writing, and he seemed surprised, but he didn't argue.

(Of course I didn't know what I was saying. He was probably right to take no notice. I was just reluctant to grow up.)

One day we were making love in the daylight, with the curtains open and sun streaming through. It was the very end of my period, which was safe, but not entirely safe. It was time for him to put a condom on, and I thought he would, but suddenly he didn't, he came inside me naked as the day, and I didn't entirely want to stop him, and I didn't stop him. Heat, blue sky, the avid spring of Portugal. We lay there, spent, in the gaze of the window, with the blank panorama, the tall chimney, the nest where small dark outlines tussled and wrestled, gaping their tiny beaks at the sky, trying to feed from the awkward white bird which hovered above them, wings sighing with longing as it beat, beat at the April air. Slowly, our breathing and heartbeats steadied; we thought we were the same as before; we dozed and dreamed and idly bickered; we might not get to the sea today. But in fact, something fundamental had happened, and we weren't drunk, and we had both assented, though the impetus, the boldness, came from him. It was the first time in seventeen years of love-making that I'd given my body the least chance of getting pregnant.

But I soon forgot. It didn't happen again.

Back home, back in the world, a lot was going on. In Iran, Jimmy Carter lost patience over US hostages and sent in a plane to get them out; the mission failed; the situation worsened. Faber accepted Nick's book, with some edits, and he started teaching in a language school. He paid for me to go to a hotel in Eastbourne to get on with a thriller I had planned, called *Grace*, whose dénouement took place in that Victorian resort. I had a narrow single room which looked over the sea, a tamer, greyer sea than Portugal's. Spring was coming, even here, but everything seemed sour and grim; I missed Nick; what I wrote was dull.

Then two critical events made us all long for dullness. In the USSR, the Chernobyl reactor released its deadly plume of radiation.

For days the news was obsessed with the disaster as wind spread the blight all over the world. It would be in berries and reindeer flesh, but also in birds' eggs, cows, milk. There seemed no way that you could escape it. Some people advocated iodine as prophylaxis; I bought it, but then read somewhere else that it was more dangerous than the radiation. I felt desperate, actually; the planet had been poisoned, the natural world that I loved so much, the glory we had just seen in Portugal. And then there was more news in hushed, urgent voices. One night America bombed Libya, and the planes had flown from bases in Britain. At night I heard engines of planes flying over, bearing down on my narrow hotel room, my single bed. It reminded me of the terrors of my girlhood. Would retaliation come our way?

And two things happened closer to home. The food at the hotel became sickening. There was too much fat in everything. I couldn't eat it. It made me sweat, though I loved my food, and I'd loved hotels since my childhood when I wished we were richer, so we needn't go camping. But I didn't feel well. The stairs made me breathless. There was definitely something wrong with me ... I must be ultra-sensitive to radiation.

Then I found a small lump on my right breast. It was there, then it wasn't, I'd imagined it; and then it was definitely there, in the morning, hard and flat, like a sequin or lentil. OK, I had cancer. Dread fear of death. How quickly Chernobyl had done for me. (In fact, it was nothing, just a fibroadenoma, a meaningless lump that goes away on its own, though of course I did not know that then.) My period came, pale and sickly, and then another just as thin and wan while I pushed myself drearily on through the novel, guiltily aware how much this stay was costing. I didn't want to worry Nick by telling him all this.

But spring, impervious to radiation, was brightening the Sussex coast. Suddenly, it seemed, the sea was blue. The corporation flower-beds bloomed overnight, a festive banner of scarlet primulas, golden daffodils, sea-blue hyacinths stretched along the front outside my window. I walked up the road towards the cliffs. I was feeling better, but still slightly breathless. The tiny, disquieting lentil was still there, but now my breasts were doing something different: they ached and were tender. It wasn't unpleasant, it was sensuous. A swelling feeling like the sea and the blossom. I felt mysteriously happy.

Something struck me. I stopped in mid-step. It couldn't be. Could it? Was it possible? I did a pregnancy test in the bleak hotel bathroom. Two clear blue lines stood like staves in two windows. They said I was pregnant. I stared at myself, an uncertain new face in the bathroom mirror. I had to take it in, now, here, alone, before I talked to Nick or my mother. Everything looked different. The words had gone missing. Two halves of a sentence came glassily together, something impossible I could not say.

I Maggie Gee. The pale face in the mirror, married but essentially still on my own. I had always been *this*. I was thirty-seven.

I Maggie Gee was going to have a baby.

12 Why do I write?

dancing

About two months before Rosa was born, the reality of caring for her came home to me. My days would change. She would always be there. How would I ever write again?

I asked another woman writer, who said, 'Don't worry. My baby slept in a basket on the floor.' Fortunately I didn't believe her, as Rosa hardly slept, in the day, from the beginning.

This baby had already revolutionised our lives. Because of her, because we had to be grown up, we were trying to buy our first property, a two-bed flat in Kensal Green, though there were problems with the freehold, and asbestos in the cupboards. Buying a flat meant we had to earn more money. Nick had acquired a desirable temporary contract as a scriptwriter at the BBC, which with luck would continue, but he wouldn't be around to look after Rosa, and I would still need to earn money of my own (it is a point of pride that since 1982, when I became a full-time writer, I have always paid my share of the bills). That meant I would have to re-energise the thriller, *Grace*, that I had slowly and dreamily completed while pregnant, longhand in a lined notebook. There was a lot to be done, but the hormones made me sleepy. With a month to go, we moved in to the flat, the first place we had had entirely to ourselves, with no live-in landlady, no shared bathroom.

(Here I need another brief aside on friendship, which will take me from 1979, when I arrived in London, to 1986, when Rosa was born. Because our former 'landlady', Grania, cannot just be called a landlady. She was a rare spirit who became a friend, her blue Georgian house full of books and paintings, an Irish intellectual who had been to Oxford and worked in a hospice because she believed in it. It was she who had said, hearing we were to get married, 'Well there is another room free, you know. Nick could have it, if you like.' It hadn't occurred to us to live together. We really were babes in the wood, I think now. I had sent this information to my aunts and uncles: 'We're going to get married, but not live together' – but of course, the root cause was, we had nowhere to live. He was renting a cupboard-sized room in Paddington, I was Grania's tenant in Camden Town. Then Grania stepped in, mild, amused, with her offer of a room on the floor above mine. Of course he would like it. Yes, yes! Would we have stayed together, had we not lived together?

Looking back, my friends have been guardian angels, though of course they were normal, human, earthbound, fallible people who saw my failings. 'You *must* know there are spaces after punctuation,' said my kind friend Tony Holden, in despair, after reading the typescript of my first novel. 'And you *can't* send envelopes like that.' (It was on its ninth or tenth tour of service, written all over, with criss-crossing PSs.) 'Maggie, pick up your purse and your gloves,' sighed Barbara, watching me scatter my possessions once again, myopically carefree, all over the floor. 'Please don't leave the light on in the kitchen,' begged Grania. 'And perhaps you could be careful not to slam the door.' 'Your letters are over the top,' said Beverly. 'You don't have to thank me so much. I don't like it.'

One summer, Grania came down to see us, her steady step on the wooden stairs. She had been thinking about the rent. We nodded, resigned. It was very low, and yet we did not earn much money. But she said, 'I've been looking at my outgoings. I thought I would put the rent down three pounds.' Twelve pounds less per month! It was a fortune to us.

Pure chance, if there's really any chance in life: I had found her through an advertisement in *Time Out*, in summer 1980. I had survived my rackety beginnings in London, working as a live-in maid in Chelsea where I was expected to dust the carpets and the lady of the house walked behind me, inspecting; the 'free basement flat' she supplied in return turned out to leak rain all over my books, and the woman was demented, and I was trapped, but my friends, Jim Stredder, Tony, Phil, emerged from the trees when I sent desperate postcards – 'I am enslaved to a madwoman' – and once again helped me, joined forces to get me out of there. Then I fell on the shambling, eccentric sweetness of Maria Iwtschenko's house in Chiswick, inhabited by elderly Russians who had been expropriated in the Revolution, and one embattled but fascinating Polish countess, where I had a green bedsit with a gas-ring and a sink, and paid the rent by doing shifts as a hotel receptionist. When Maria Iwtschenko, by now in her eighties, had to sell the house, I spotted the ad that Grania had placed.

Large sunny room would suit quiet person. I turned up for the interview looking unfeasibly unquiet, in cream jacket and trousers with a shocking pink tie, pink belt, pink earrings, and bright pink socks which were the icing on the cake, a very pink, very creamy cake. I was shy, in fact, but I hid it well.

Grania looked at me, and seemed to quite like me. She asked me if I was 'very sociable', a question perhaps aimed at all that pinkness (I was blind, I think, to the effect of my clothes, which were curiously at odds with my real habits, which were, indeed, mostly scholarly and quiet. I didn't see people for days on end; I read voraciously; I wrote.) I was finishing a PhD, I told her. She already had one, on nineteenth-century literature. She overlooked the pink. She let me in.

On our improvised wedding day, which nobody knew about but Grania (that is, except for Barbara, our bridesmaid, and John Waite, the best man), she left two presents in the kitchen: a large white hat – it was blazing August – and a beautiful unorthodox wedding cake, a sponge cake covered with strawberries and peaches. When we returned from Cambridge we were the house's young marrieds, an exception to the other female poets and students. I am sure we were sometimes noisy and annoying, because two people together laugh and chatter a lot, and there are lovers' quarrels, which is worse, and two typewriters rattled on different floors, but she knew that we loved her, and the tall blue house, and the garden she had garlanded with old-fashioned roses, pale pink, cream, white, Gertrude Jekyll style, among tall blue delphiniums and fragile harebells, and in the morning, she would stand there among them, watching things emerge, weeding, thinking, with her large blue thoughtful eyes and thick hair. 'Every time you make love, it is a sacrament,' she said.

She had nothing in common with a landlady.)

But now it was 1986, I was pregnant, and a baby wouldn't suit the tiny shared shower room in the basement, and its crying certainly wouldn't be quiet. Now once again they emerged from the wings, my cast of friends, and helped us to move. I had become very worried about our books. I was far too unwieldy to pack or unpack them. The new flat, now stripped of both damp and asbestos, was in many ways delightful, but had no bookshelves. Nick seemed very busy doing who knows what. I was busy growing, slow and sleepy. For the first time in my life, I was probably restful. I swam in hormones. I let things be.

On the evening of the move, he took me over to the flat. I was eight months pregnant and expected to find chaos. Instead, I found the front room completely shelved up, with the books all installed in alphabetical order, and standing in front of them, the friends who had helped with electric drills, know-how, muscle. Musa, Campbell, Barbara. I cheered, they cheered, we drank to each other. There is a picture of me standing, curved out like a pear, by a wall of books, crying with happiness.

But I knew that *Grace*, the novel I was writing, didn't work. No one had told me, no one had read it, but I couldn't fail to see the plot was becalmed, I fell asleep when I tried to read it; and the narrative hadn't even managed to climb from the leisure of my notebooks into the viability of typescript; it was dull, dull, that was the truth, and the baby was coming, and I wasn't ready, except for the physical act of birth, which I'd tried to prepare for with classes and yoga. Would there be a life beyond the birth? If so, I had no idea how to live it. I phoned Brent Childcare Services in a panic. A calm voice told me about child-minders. I only needed to know they were there. Now I could face the great adventure.

But why did I feel, even at that point, that I would cease to exist if I couldn't go on writing? Why have I always needed to write? In a way, it has always defined my life. It made me think I could never have children; I accepted it; I had to be a writer. I wrote poetry from infants' school onwards. It's as if I had signed up to some cult at six. In my last long vacation from Oxford, I wrote my first novel, in a four-week monastic burst of activity, up in the attic of a chalet in Switzerland my parents had rented with my father's brother, the very first time we hadn't gone camping. I wrote it, really, by arithmetic. This is the meaning of 'Ignorance is bliss.' I thought, 'The average novel is 100,000 words long,' and divided that sum by the available days (25), so wrote 4,000 words a day, because that was what was needed to get it done, though it did seem to mean an awful lot of work, and left me no time to reread what I had written.

My father had given me a 'can-do' attitude. I'm grateful to him. For all my naïvety, for all the weaknesses of what I poured out, something important had been achieved. I remember the happiness of the last day, when I had dotted the 'i's of the last sentence, and walked up with Aunty Hilda through the pines to the resort of Montana Vermala, where we bought exotic food to entertain the others. How game Hilda was, Dad's younger brother's wife, a trait which perhaps helped her live into her nineties, surviving all the brothers and all the other wives. Our one rule on that happy day was: 'Buy food that none of us has eaten before.' I remember only vine leaves stuffed with rice, which were unknown in Britain in 1969. I was utterly happy as we climbed down the mountain with bags full of oily, alien food. I was queen of the earth. I was a novelist, now, because I'd written a novel.

And there's some truth to the idea that getting to the end was all that mattered. With novels, it's the length that kills, as Robert Louis Stevenson remarked, and I'd proved I had the drive and the stamina to do it. Then, in my twenties, as I added degrees – an Oxford BLitt, the PhD – and between them, worked two years in publishing, I struggled to keep writing in the gaps. I wrote long narrative poems, tried out novellas. In a six-month interlude 'on the dole' between leaving publishing and moving to Wolverhampton to start a doctorate, I wrote, in an isolated cottage in Oxford, the book that would become my first published novel, an 'experimental thriller' called *Dying in Other Words*. I had a half-formed thought, from the depth of my innocence: *I think this will win me the Booker Prize*. But the two publishers I sent it to did not agree, though one of them asked me out to lunch, and said, in effect, he would probably publish if I would cut the last third of the book, a bizarre section of poems and prose supposedly written by my heroine, Moira.

Cut? I was shocked. Of course I would not. I was on the high horse of my higher degrees, and practical concerns were nothing to me. Nor did I understand what was obvious: you must keep sending books out, again and again. I somehow just felt my day would come.

And five years later, thanks (once again) to a friend (which one? I still don't know) who told a publisher I had something worth seeing, a small publisher in Sussex, Harvester Press, wrote me a letter asking to see the manuscript, 'with a view to finding the statue in the stone'.

Cheek! 'Send us your rubbish, and we'll turn it into art.' But I posted the manuscript, which had only been greying and wrinkling in some corner, and forgot all about it when there was no response.

Six months later, a letter came offering a £500 advance to publish it. I learned much later that the manuscript had been read by that great man and novelist, David Hughes, author of *The Little Book*, who liked my strange tale, and recommended publication. Without him, who's to say I would have continued? He didn't reveal the role he had played until some years after we got to know each other in the mid-1990s. My first book, so odd and passionate, might have gone to a dozen other readers, but David was there at the crossroads, unseen, and gave me the secret benediction of luck. It had happened again: the universe split, and in the one I remember, I received the right letter.

I was amazed when I opened the envelope. I read it again and again for the catch. I called up my brother, and he, his girlfriend Liz and I sat out on Chiswick Green, under a sunset sky, and celebrated in the summer evening with a bottle of wine. We were, all three, as amazed as each other. I was clearly never, ever, going to get published. Then suddenly I was. And now we were here. The impossible was all about me: a crimson glory sinking into brilliant indigo, the dark grass stretching away into the trees where every mystery might be waiting for me, the lights of passing cars winging over our faces, the stars of happiness steadying above, becoming clearer and more confident.

I came out in July, when few books were published, and got 'rave reviews', the kind that welcome a new arrival. Thanks to my friend Tony Holden, who was deputy editor, *The Times* ran a full page extract. A team of judges who included Brian Aldiss and Hermione Lee put me in the top twelve of the Booker submissions, on what would now be called the Booker longlist. My luck seemed to grow exponentially, as if it had seeded in the dark of delay through the seven years the book was confined in its drawer, and had burst out, shining and fat, a pale puffball. I got a letter from Robert McCrum at Faber, declaring himself a huge fan of the novel and saying how delighted he would be to read anything I liked to send him. (What did I do with it? Did I write back? No, I was paralysed as well as delighted. My heart beat too fast. I put it in a frame.) I was included in the list of twenty 'Best of Young British Writers', the original one with Martin Amis, Pat Barker, William Boyd, Buchi Emecheta, Kazuo Ishiguro, Adam Mars-Jones, Ian McEwan, Philip Norman, Graham Swift, Rose Tremain, AN Wilson and other famous names. I was blonde, young for that group, photogenic, though in fact photo sessions were agony. In ninety per cent of the shots I would look taut and nervous, but a lucky few caught me beginning to smile at the absurd novelty of being half-famous. *The Times* sent a photographer to take my portrait, and spread it, huge, beside their two-page feature on our group. (It must have been annoying. I had only published one novel. But I revelled in that fifteen minutes in the sun.) Then I was awarded the prestigious University of East Anglia Writing Fellowship, against stiff competition that included Andrew Motion. I was suddenly shooting down the rapids, though I didn't have a clue how to steer the canoe. I got an agent, Mark Hamilton, who took charge. My next novel, *The Burning Book*, was bought by Faber for the sum of £4,500; the third, *Light Years*, for £10,000.

But by then, I was starting to break the rules. I was living with a man. I was happy with him. I wasn't always alone, reading and writing. I ate meals with Nick, instead of a book. I got married, and my agent worried, and my publisher sent Nick around the world to write his book about Robert Louis Stevenson.

In a way, things were going swimmingly. Suddenly I had love, work and money, only a couple of years after a thirtieth birthday made bleak by my sense that I had none of them. But in another breath, there were problems ahead, and I hadn't the experience to see them, or avoid them. Four years in, then five years in, my magnificent puffball of luck seemed to expire in a slow soft sigh of missing increments. I wasn't winning prizes, while the peers who joined Faber not long before me – Peter Carey, Kazuo Ishiguro – had won, or been shortlisted for, the Booker. Faber made less effort with the paperback of *Light Years* than they had promised in a florid memo which mentioned dump-bins and national tours. (So what? I would think now, but I was young and headstrong, and believed the enormous praise I had received, and took it for granted that, if I was good, I would automatically get sales and prizes.) How young I was. How very foolish. And the family trait of anger let me down. Anger and rashness, which you could call passion, but self-righteousness also, which makes us all blind. I quarrelled with Robert, and left my agent, swayed by what I now think was largely empty praise from a youngish female agent who approached me at some 'Best of Young British' jamboree and said she thought I was 'the bees' knees'. (Meaning what? Perhaps nothing. But I thought she would dust me with the pollen of money.)

These days I get on with publishers. I haven't argued with them for a decade, except for the odd callisthenic textual wrangle that invigorates the editor-writer relationship. But in those days I argued, and Robert wrote a letter saying goodbye when Rosa was not many months old, and *Grace* was still languishing in notebooks. The timing was dreadful, just after childbirth. Everything was suddenly uncertain. I didn't like the novel I had written while pregnant, and yet I had no time to rewrite it. I had a new agent, but no publisher. I was thirty-eight, potentially a dangerous age, although I believed I would be young for ever, though I still looked young, and slimmer than before as I ran around Rosa, and (quite soon) after her.

And here I am still, running around the subject, avoiding the nub of the question I asked – writing and Rosa: Rosa and writing. Before Rosa, writing. Why write? Why Rosa? How in heaven's name could I have both? I have been kicking up dust for several pages, unable to touch the heart of things.

I have to write because I have to speak. Most genuine art is a break for freedom, a run into the light, evading the warders. Then craft comes in, refining, restraining, but the initial impulse is usually rebellion, the will to bring something new into the world. In the home I grew up in, too much was not spoken, or was dangerous to speak, suppressed and diverted. This is normal, of course. There are taboos and customs.

The custom in our house was, defer to the male. My father always had the last word. My brother John, being four years older, and very brilliant, knew more than me, and must have had more say, though that's simplifying – he also represented more of a challenge to my father, which sometimes made his position precarious. My younger brother arrived when I was nine, so he wasn't really part of the original family that established my sense of the universe I lived in, and my place in it as the youngest and most fearful. For the taboos in our house were backed up by fear, and once the fear was removed, once I had fled the coop and the old cock could no longer harry his flock, I wrote irrepressibly and joyously. And in social life, I couldn't bear to be talked down; still can't, to the cost of many talkative men who assume women only want to sit and listen. I like to listen, very much, I like to ask questions and learn from the answers, but I sometimes like to speak, as well, and sometimes I'm not ready to stop speaking. 'Leave it,' was my father's way of closing subjects where we disagreed with him, or upset him. But he couldn't tell me to leave my writing. He didn't know I was doing it. And when he read things I had written, poems or stories, he praised them and encouraged me, not seeing that one day this precocious skill would enable me to write about the family, not seeing that I was acquiring the tools I needed to tunnel my way out into the open.

Though the nature of writing is always two-edged: it frees you, but it makes you work to excess. The novel is far too long, as a form, but still too short and too unyielding to relive your own life and make it right. The book suddenly takes off somewhere else, on its own. It makes a dash for the future as well as the past. It grows bored with the self, and seeks otherness. So I never quite found the infinite terrain where I could reinvent and absolve myself. But I think that's the impulse, I think that's why I do it. And yet the ground always falls away, the truth is not quite there, the door's only half-open.

It is not your own life, though it is your own life. I can't climb inside, yet so much of me is there.

My books are more me than anything else. That means 'more *of* me' not 'more *to* me'; I could never say my work was more to me than Rosa or Nick; in the old conundrum, 'What do you save from the burning library, the irreplaceable books or the abandoned baby?', I could not save the books when the baby was crying. Yet the books, my books, matter more to my ego, to the frail-tough wavering stalk of me that holds me to the light where I can live in the world, have a husband, child, friends, 'normality'. Maybe books allowed me to have my baby, made me stable enough to hold someone else. In that sense, the books I have written are me. They are better than me, less flawed, less impassioned, less swayed by brief feelings of hurt or anger, more able to see other human beings from their own point of view, rather than as the source of personal wounds or blessings which they can turn into in the shock of the moment, the shocking rawness of everyday life. Books are more accurate, more beautiful, less messy. And they waste no time; instead, they save it. I hate wasting time. Time is precious. My twelve books, piled pell mell on the shelf, have made something solid from the time flashing past: and with this one, there will be thirteen.

(For the first time, now my own life is stage centre. Am I straining to turn my best profile to the light?)

I write to reinvent, to impose order. To make the world outside the book bearable. To say there can be more than the violent chaos that sometimes washed about me when I was growing up. To tell the world what I think of it, too, to answer back: *this is me, I see you*. It was the same thing, really, long, long ago, when around the age of five I tacitly asserted that I could do more than copy the words on the blackboard, adding writing of my own to my first school 'Writing' books. I was a law-abiding girl; and yet there I was, writing, working inwards from the back pages of the notebook to meet the 'official' pages at the front, mostly rhyming 'poems' I thought I invented, as the first poet in the history of my world, pairing fish and dish, cat and mat.

A teacher must have read it and added silver stars, for when I found it as an adult, there they were, not much greyed by the years, on the edge of the pages. I cannot gauge how important that was. Would I have gone on if no one had noticed? Would I have kept writing if I'd never got published? In its origin, there's only that urge to rebellion, a drive to make things new that pushes everyone away; but soon the young rebel wants someone else to notice. Someone did, thank God, and saw something in me. Something that linked me to all creation, something that allowed me to love myself. I think creativity exists in everyone, but many people never have the luck that I did, to chance upon a smile of acceptance or permission.

For me, rhymes clinched things, comforted, released like a chord on the piano when the elements are right and the pedal lifts, leaving the faintest, most satisfying silvery ring. I did not know what I needed to write: the act itself was what mattered to me.

It was like dancing. Yes, it was joy. I was on my own, I was free, I was dancing. The words were my own, my secret music. I learned what I needed to survive and be happy.

No wonder I was frightened, before Rosa was born. Would it be a transaction, her life for mine? My mother told me later that my father had said, 'Perhaps Margaret won't need to write any more.' In fact, I needed to write more than ever. The miracle was, it was possible. I found a child-minder five houses down the street – her name was Daphne, and she had high standards; 'her' mothers boasted that the children came home with a new painting every day. I noticed they were worryingly quiet at table. But Rosa only went there for two and a half hours a day, and because she was tiny, Daphne carried her around in a baby-carrier on her chest, and I expressed milk into a bottle so that if she woke up, Daphne could feed her. Two and a half hours, from ten to twelve-thirty!

It was enough for me to make a start. Because Rosa still slept in a cot by our bed, I could write in the room that would one day be hers, a nice, bright room with a big pile of cushions, a square table with a red tablecloth. The sash-window looked out on the narrow pathway that led from the back door to the garden. A glimpse of green lawn, clematis, lilac, a sunlit space that I worked towards.

Time was short and infinitely precious. The milky, dreamy hormones were ebbing. I read through the slow, unstructured manuscript I had written in a trance while I was pregnant, and rewrote it ruthlessly, straight to typescript, without looking at what I had done before, in lean, quick, cinematic sections that reflected my newly urgent schedule. By the time Rosa was one, I had a novel to sell, and although for two harrowing weeks at the end she turned away from me to her father, her little plump arms pointing to the truth, that he had more to give her than her wild-eyed mother, fingers hammering the keys as I raced to finish, she soon forgave me when life returned to normal. The novel went to auction, and Heinemann bought it for two and a half times what I had earned before.

The money mattered, but the book mattered more. I was still a writer, but I had a daughter. I was still a writer, *and I had a daughter*. She was plump and healthy, with a high round forehead, wide-spaced blue eyes that grew green later, a cheery, chattering way with people and a desire for perpetual motion. Rosa: Rosa. A new person. We fell in love with her as soon as we saw her. The flat was held together by a sunny corridor that ran from our bedroom to the high front room. As Nick or I carried Rosa up and down it, we kissed her big scantily-curled head so often I am surprised there was any hair left.

We pass it still, that first flat where we lived for the first five

Rosa, solid and warm in my hands

years of Rosa's life. I feel versions of us must still live there, somehow, ghostly avatars of happiness. As soon as we started to want her, she came, between two hot wing-beats of time, in Portugal, and then she was with us, and we were three. Shadows came later to teach us better, but we knew even then her first year was miraculous, that we had never been happier, that we could never be happier, as we held her, solid and warm, in our hands. This was the space of bodily bliss.

Above my head, though, there was still the high wire, glittering in its own cold light. I left Rosa with Daphne, and hurried to climb it, two hours left, then an hour and a half, and in the last half-hour, the world fell away, I forgot to worry, I became the writing, I was on my own, and I danced along it, I cut away the dullness, I found my nerve.

13 My animal luck (vi)

*Rosa is young
and we grow older*

The poet EJ Scovell, who I knew as Joy, and her husband CS Elton, who was Charles to me, author of *The Patterns of Animal Behaviour* and the founder of British ecology, became friends of mine in my very early twenties when their niece Liza married my elder brother John. (And this was the alchemy that occurred when the State invested in its working classes by giving bright children a top-flight education: untapped talent was brought up into the light. My brother and I were translated to Oxford, and married into the educated middle classes.) Joy and Charles were nearly half a century older than me, but it was so interesting, their tall Park Town house covered in red and green creeper; the books, the ideas; the endless murmur of conversation about voles or daisies, odes and dactyls. Charles influenced my thinking about the web of life; he helped me to see human beings as one species in a vast and complex net of animals and plants, and I saw, in his relationship with Joy, that art could marry science, that both were forms of restless curiosity, feeding the same attempt to understand the world. They remained two of my dearest friends until they died, in their nineties, near the end of the century. How kind they were to me when I was young and raw.

I learned that the old could remain youthful. They had brought up two children, Rob and Katy, and had a vivid love for their grandchildren, some of whom lived on Montserrat, and were half-Caribbean. All children touched Joy's imagination as a poet. Some of her best and most anthologised poems are about children and the passage of time (she is also the poet of old age, one of the best in our language). In a poem called 'At the school gate', she muses on the young parents she sees picking up their children at the end of the day. They are:

> *Still beautiful, but not in that first way –*
> *their used and hardy beauty is in fruit today.*

As the mother of a baby, you can't be a child; nor can you and your husband be children together (though that comes back later, when the babies are older and need less to be done for them just to stay alive, so you can sometimes, briefly, all be children together). But at first, parents are servants. There are a lot of dull things to be done. Large plastic objects must be brought into the house. You can't travel light, walking swiftly through the streets enjoying the feel of air on your face. You are struggling with the child, pushchair, nappies, bottles, toys, changing-mat. You are bulkier and slower; you start to look older. You think less about your looks, and become 'used and hardy'.

I thought about beauty in the world outside, even more than before, perhaps, as I tried to show it to Rosa, her wide pale eyes looking up at me, and beyond me, the clouds (I didn't realise she could see it for herself) – but after the beginning, when I was relieved to be slim again after pregnancy, I had less time and energy than ever in my life to think about my own appearance. The photos of me at the time attest it. I didn't care, I knew Nick loved me. But I aged five years, perhaps, in two. And when Rosa was three, illness struck.

First-generation RSI or Repetitive Strain Injury, the occupational hazard that came upon the users, or over-users, of the first basic computers. Two giant boxes had arrived at Christmas: an Amstrad computer, a digital printer, presents from Nick to help me write.

Perched on a rackety upright chair at a too-high desk, typing on tip-toe in our bedroom, ignoring the strange creeping pins and needles in my arms and legs and the gathering heaviness in my neck and shoulders, I had worked like a madwoman, 4,000 words a day, 7,000 words a day, *10,000 words a day*, on the final day I wrote 10,000 words, for the new machine encouraged madness, my hands burning eagerly over the keyboard, eyes dry, cheeks hot, powering on to the end of my novel, *Where are the Snows*. The day after I finished, my limbs started swelling, my joints seized up. In a terrifying whole-body manifestation of distress I could no longer write, nor brush my teeth, nor walk. I thought I was dying, but I was diagnosed with a strange new syndrome that was puzzling doctors: RSI. No one knew what to do. I tried doctors, NHS and private, physiotherapists, acupuncturists. All that helped was rest, as one doctor had told me, but it went against my nature to accept it. Every nerve in my body felt angrily electric, so acupuncture was a torment. Physiotherapy at least gave me something I could do for myself; a little group of exercises, but oh, so very little; the movements I could make without pain were so few. Would it ever get better? No one knew. I had done this to myself, by neglecting my body, by forgetting I had an animal life, by thinking I could chain myself to a machine. The forgotten body had grown hurt and angry. Now I would have to be afraid of it. I was slow, and careful, and hoped it would forgive me.

The worst of it passed within six months, but I could not run or even walk as I used to, and my outline softened, and my head was too heavy, bending forward to avoid pain. For a year or so, I couldn't even carry a handbag; it hurt us both that I could not carry Rosa; my muscles must have weakened, and I suppose my bones.

I did not mind too much, because I had my family, my little unit that had to survive, and much more to think about than my body. And there was so much happiness when Rosa was young.

I can't write a 'miserable mum memoir'. Yes, I was tired, and I got things wrong, and sometimes I must have hated her because she would not go to sleep – you can't negotiate, or bribe, or order; she was herself, intransigent, and I ran against the rock face in myself; *our needs were opposed*; and hers had to win, but still, it made me furious. Or I hated myself for leaving her with the child-minder so I could work; and sometimes I got behind with the writing even though I knew I had short-changed my daughter, and felt 'I'm no good as a mother, and no good as a writer.' Once when Rosa was two and a bit I picked her up from her nursery late, and when she got home she cried with rage and went under the table in her room, stopped crying but would not come out, and said, 'I don't want you to work any more, Mummy. Don't work any more.' The words that I most dreaded to hear, but the next day she seemed to have forgotten it, she went to nursery school, I was not late.

On good days, I felt the most radiant gratitude: something amazing had been given me, and I didn't seem to have paid the price. One winter afternoon when she was still quite small, I vividly remember hurrying to get her from her child-minder, after an afternoon when work had gone well: she was happy to see me: big gap-toothed smile; I hurried back home with her in her pushchair, eager to get her home and cuddle her, but a moon appeared in the cool blue sky, very thin and frail, growing clearer, whiter. 'Oh look, Rosa, there's the moon.' Of course she was staring at it already. 'Moon,' she said, 'Moon, Mummy,' and every so often, as we sprinted through the twilight, past terraced houses and ugly cars, a pale thin mother with her pale round daughter, gazing at each other, and up at the moon, though I also had to think about the cars and the people, she said, 'Moon, Mummy', or 'Mummy, moon', and I felt I was part of an enormous happiness.

Rosa had made me part of the world. *I was allowed to work and have a baby.*

I talk about the hard bits because I feel I ought to; I don't want to give an unreal picture; but my overriding feeling was that life had begun. A rich new life; we had started again.

Rosa was fiercely individual from the start. Lifted out of the bath, at around twenty months, and planted beside it on her own two feet, with a towel around her, she said, triumphant, 'I'm a person!' – that essential knowledge some people never find. And again, I suppose at around the same age, when she was at the other end of a room where her father and I were complaining about her, half-humorously, half-seriously, for at a very early stage of toilet training she started hiding faeces round the room, and I had just found them, three little dried corms (it was like a joke she was playing on us) – she remarked, loudly indignant, to the wall, 'But I'm a *wonderful* child.' Maybe we had told her that too often, but she was a wonder, and we wondered at her, this child who came to us so late. Yet her dazzling youth certainly made us older (for some reason, I think men feel this more. I have heard two men – though not my husband – explain that alongside the love they felt for their first child was the sense that they had been evicted from Eden; it's the child's turn now; they are displaced.)

But Nick and I were closer than ever. I remember the absurd thought that came, the night we came home from the hospital. Nick's face was beside me on the pillow again, and Rosa was at the foot of the bed, briefly asleep, in a Moses basket. 'I love him because he is *so like Rosa*,' I thought as I gazed, amazed, at his face. It was a back-to-front thought; of course *she* was like *him*, so like that their young photos could easily be confused; but I was stunned by the way in which my world had come together, for Nick, to me, was the infinitely lovable image of the baby, my new love-object.

All her life Rosa has been fun, and funny. Left to have supper, aged five or six, with our friend Fatima and her family, she did not eat all her food. 'Why aren't you eating your meat?' said Fatima. 'I don't want to be a fat bastard,' said Rosa. And the 'stranger danger' lessons at school bore fruit the teacher may not have intended. Rosa told us what they had been learning that day. Nick asked her, 'So what would you do if a man stopped his car and offered you sweeties?' 'I would say "Bugger off!"' she said firmly.

She was thoughtful, as well, with her own point of view. Sometimes she helped me see how to be a mother. One day I picked her up from her nursery school – a Montessori school she loved. (Bizarrely, for the most part, and despite frank criticisms of their foibles, she ended up loving all her schools, which made me feel shifty when I discussed school with mothers who were discontented. They obviously thought I was in denial, or simply failing to play the game, the great mother-game of criticising. The bottom line was, I was grateful to the schools. Without them, I would be home educating.) In any case, that day I picked Rosa up with a pushchair, so she must have been small, not much more than three, for as soon as we could, I dispensed with it. That day I had not managed to switch off my worries about my work before I went to meet her. I was chattering away to her, on automatic pilot, about the dilemmas of my day. We were pushing down The Avenue, a long straight road. I suppose I might have wittered on for ever.

Suddenly a little voice piped up. At first I could not believe my ears.

'Big people can't be friends with little people.'

'What did you say?' I looked at her suspiciously, her round clever head, her golden curls, her wide-set green eyes like an alien's. Her cushiony lips had definitely moved.

'BIG PEOPLE CAN'T BE FRIENDS WITH LITTLE PEOPLE.'

She was looking at me, not unkindly, but as if she had made a definite statement. Yes, she had said it. I had been told. I was ashamed, yet also delighted with her. Of course it was true, and I took note. Children don't need to know adults' worries.

I have already said that I lap up advice. One of the most useful things about motherhood was said to me by someone I didn't know well. She had a daughter, too, rather older than mine, and we were worrying aloud about their happiness. 'One problem is over-identifying,' she said. 'My daughter just got fed up with me worrying and said to me, "Mum, I'm fine, honestly, I'm *not like* you, remember that!"'

I over-identified with Rosa. Of course, because although she looked like her father, with Nick's small nose and curly hair, parts of her brain were uncannily like mine. Music, for example. A marvellous surprise. It has proved to be a never-ending groundswell of pleasure that we like exactly the same music. By this I don't mean certain genres, certain composers, I mean we love the same notes and phrases. The same bar will trigger the same emotions. I can only believe this is coded, somehow, in deep folds of the emotional brain, because the response is so immediate and instinctive. Hearing something together, it speaks to us, and we often touch hands and look away, because a moment of such absolute intimacy has just come upon us. A flash of mirrors from far away, an unreasonable happiness hushing us like shyness (though at other times it makes us dance on the landing). When she sends me music, it is simple bliss.

And yet, in other ways we're totally different. Hurray for that! Hurray for difference! Hurray for the things that our children can do that we could never in a lifetime manage! The miracle of the dance of the genes, throwing up unlikeness as much as sameness.

She is sociable, very, and I am not, has always had a lot of friends, except for a brief puzzling period when she was in Year 2 of her primary school, the local school, one hundred yards down the road. Because my own junior school years had often been miserable and lonely, I had a special reason to be anxious about this.

One night she said, 'I didn't have anyone to play with, today at break time,' and I said, trying not to show my heart was sinking, 'I expect you will tomorrow.' But this refrain became more frequent, usually just as I was leaving her bedroom at night, after reading to her. 'I didn't have anyone to play with at break time.' Of course it is possible that she knew this would halt me in my tracks and bring me back for another ten minutes, but still I know it was genuine. A little stone of misery from my own past arc-ed through the evening and landed in my chest. *Rosa would be lonely, as I had been.* My own fatal unpopularity, which I had felt deeply as unlikeability, must have somehow been transmitted to her. It was all my fault. I felt wretched, and helpless. My lovely, pretty, laughing girl would be unhappy. The curse had come upon her, she had not escaped.

In fact, it was just a phase, and soon over. Never before, or since, did Rosa lack friends. I was over-reacting, over-deducing, because I over-identified.

Recently we reminisced about that time. Perhaps it was that the children were at the age where they started to notice difference, and she was different, one of only three white girls in her class. She said, 'I got something good out of it, though, because I had to find something to do in the playground, and I worked out how to fly. If you did a leap, and then another leap, and a leap upon that leap, you would fly. And I used to go round the playground trying it out.' And I said, 'But that's just like me! Because I didn't want anyone to know how lonely I was at the village school, when we moved to Watersfield, I used to walk about the playground very fast, on my own, from one side to another, looking business-like, pretending I was going somewhere.'

And she said, but laughing, 'That is sad. Sorry, Mum, you're not like me.'

In ways that I don't, she believes she can fly. She can walk into a room without anxiety. She expects to be liked, and mostly people like her. For that she can thank Nick as well as herself, the luck of his sociable, confident genes.

Now she has a bewildering number of friends. Somehow she has kept some junior school friends, and all her big group of grammar school friends, and has made a new cast of university friends, and another lot from the time she spent in Paris, and another lot, when she was living in Granada ...

I couldn't cope with Rosa's Bacchanalian procession, the constant flashing of electronic signals, texts and messages and flickering facebooks, drinks and dances, travelling, feasting, for she's also become an imaginative cook after years of only eating white bread and pasta, using every kind of vegetable, meat and fish, always trying new dishes on people she loves. Which is sometimes us, so we are lucky. Her life is like a lake I once saw in Uganda, up in the hills, deep water spread with green leaves and pink flowers, entirely covered in water-lilies, a wondrous tangle of youthful faces, bright and specific in the morning light, where one is always opening, another closing.

(And on them she smiles: but on us she scowls, for we are her parents, and now things have changed, for we are no longer the centre of her universe, the sun and moon of the adoring small child. Now she is big, and we are just the parents. We say boring things, like 'Have you got any washing?' or 'What time is your train?' or 'Did you put my jacket back in the cupboard?' or 'Stand up straight, darling. Then you're beautiful.' Thus do the old parents oppress their offspring, and she fights back, because she can. 'Are you trying to be funny, Mum?' 'BO-ring!!' or 'Pressure, pressure, you always give me pressure,' or 'It's none of your business.' 'Leave me ALONE!' The same-sex pair have the harder time, for fathers tend to adore and offer lifts, whereas mothers afflict daughters, and daughters mothers, as they try to find two different ways of being women. Both members of the dyad know the link cannot be broken, but on bad days it feels, to her and to me, as if a heavy mini-me is jammed on our shoulders. Mine stares round into my face, kvetching and complaining. 'Mum! Mu-u-m!' 'Rosa! *Rosa!*' She is me, I am her, but we have to be other. And then suddenly my big girl says something funny, or I kiss her cheek, and we are in each other's arms, she is taller than me but we dance down the hall, and her kisses hit air because I have grown smaller; seconds later, she flies through the door and has vanished.)

'Read a book,' I say. 'Do you ever read a book?' or 'Do you think you should stay in tonight and sort out your room?' But secretly I'm pleased that Rosa is so busy.

Nick and I have – do we? – (we have to say goodbye, because she has to go away into her adult life) – a lovely grownup daughter. She is twenty-two now, and has just been abroad for the third year of her languages degree at Durham. She is tall and strong and beautiful (when she stands up straight) – a *jeune fille en fleur*, full of jokes and ideas, writing songs and articles, road-running, cooking. But I haven't stopped worrying: that is the cost. I thought I had mysteriously escaped it, but love extends the surface area of your skin. You can soak up more light, you can be endlessly surprised, but you are also more vulnerable.

When she was abroad, if she was quiet, had she been abducted? My heart leaped when the Skype symbol flickered at the bottom of my computer screen and her dear, her pixillated face appeared, her laughing mouth and high, wide forehead, or just a Skype message, when the screen didn't work or she had just got up and didn't want me to know it, 'are you there, madre?' brief, no capitals, but presaging a mutual helter-skelter of words, surreal jokes, gossip, confessions – or I open my email and see the capitals: R RANKIN-GEE. Hurray, hurray.

I only want her to be all right. If she is all right, and Nick is all right, my basic emotional tripod is steady.

I posted her parcels of porridge to Spain. 'Mum don't worry, I'm *fine*,' she said. She throws back smiles, insults, garlands, but like life itself, she has come and gone, my beautiful girl, my heart, my Rosa. We stay where we are, and they go on.

'If the meaning of an animal's life is movement ...'

The illness passed also, the RSI, the visit of old age with which this chapter began. I was grateful when I could write again, longhand, slowly, and fetch a little shopping, though even one light plastic carrier could bring the pain in my shoulders back. The wonder is, the body tends to get better from everything that will not kill it, and very slowly, I did get better, and movement came back, the joy of movement. I started swimming. I was running again.

But something had happened to my work. I had taken it for granted, perhaps, my luck, and luck must never be taken for granted. Life was too busy. I grew too busy. Nick was successful, at the BBC, and the price of success was making many features, ambitious features involving travel, and other programmes which, his craftsmanship insisted, could not be made in the time allotted. He had to work evenings, and sometimes weekends. My agent had encouraged me to leave Heinemann in search of more money, and negotiated a sizeable advance, a £75,000 two-book contract, with Jonathan Warner, the young head of HarperCollins's literary fiction list, Flamingo. *Lost Children* came out in 1994. Now it was time to write the second. But Jonathan had committed suicide, leaving a wife and daughter, not long after *Lost Children* was published, a dreadful piece of news that hit everyone hard. The RSI had slowed my production, and Nick couldn't help with Rosa very often. I was left, in the end, with less than six months to write and deliver the second novel. I went too fast. I rushed it. I fluffed it. The book I delivered, called at that stage *The Keeper of the Gate*, but eventually *The White Family*, would one day bring me great satisfaction, but unwisely, I submitted something less than perfect.

It was unlike me; I am a control freak, and I know that my work is not ordinary, not universally pleasing or lovable, and so needs the armour-plating of technique. *Do not let yourself be vulnerable.*

But it's hopeless advice. We're all vulnerable. Tread carefully, young writers in the literary jungle.

14 My animal luck (vii)

the literary jungle

In retrospect, I can see that what happened was a motorway pile-up: too many causes. Two years earlier, researching *Lost Children*, I made some visits to a centre for the homeless in east London, and sat in on their group therapy sessions. Many of the stories stretched back to childhood; one man had been sexually abused in a Catholic children's home; one woman abandoned by schizophrenic parents. But more of them had foundered in middle age, when too many things went wrong at once. Within the same few months, a relationship ended, they were made redundant, illness struck, they were declared bankrupt. And they fell through the net. They were worryingly like all the people I knew; they had no special tragic flaw.

I saw it in theory, then I learned it in practice.

1995: a watershed. I was forty-six; Rosa was eight. My agent had moved to Canada; I was passed on to the excellent managing director of the same agency, who was known as a good agent, and a gentleman, but the truth was, he had not specifically *chosen* me, and inheritance did not seem the safest route. (Yet my editor at HarperCollins, too, had inherited me, after the death of the editor who chose me. I should have seen the signs, I should have seen the danger, but I lived day to day, *writing, Rosa, Rosa, writing*, pell mell, myopic.) I was very ambitious, am ambitious still. It felt as though this was make or break. I was on my way to fifty. I had to get up there.

It's hard to recreate all the reasons for the crash. If I had a tragic flaw, it was arrogance, which sounds like ignorance, and came from it. I simply thought I could do what I wanted. If you don't come from a literary background, perhaps it takes you longer to learn the rules? And I had stayed curiously isolated. Even though I had been one of the 'Best of Young British', even though I had been a Booker judge, I had mostly stayed at home with Nick and Rosa, writing books and getting on with my life. *I thought that the writing was all you had to do.* It seems extraordinary, looking back at it now, but I'd probably been to less than a dozen literary parties, all told. I didn't see that they were important. I see it now; you get out there and smile, and meet people, and are seen on the circuit, which means you are recognised as 'one of us'. Moreover, you learn lessons from the group. I should have attended to a stray remark Jonathan Warner made when he paid so well for me: 'I love your work, but I was surprised, when I asked around the office, some people hadn't heard of you.' I wasn't on the circuit. I remained naïve, and my thought processes don't bear examination.

Perhaps, now Jonathan was dead, I should move from HarperCollins, even though I was in the middle of a two-book contract? I had no personal links there any more, and I'd heard of people doing just that. We would get a big advance, and pay them off (yet advances, all round, were too big, in the '80s. I saw the crest building, I didn't see the crash.) I had moved before, I could move again (but you can't keep moving on for ever. Too many moves give you a bad reputation.) Yes, I felt my age meant I had to climb, but I hadn't considered it was also a drawback. I thought I was still seen as a young contender. At forty-six, it was a dangerous assumption.

I approached the tallest, and said to be the toughest, agent with a literary reputation. His name had lustre because of his clients, yet the offices were small and uncomfortable and hard to get to, and I never felt at ease. Personally we were ill-assorted; he was too tall, too aristocratic, too dry, too shy, with an amused, conspiratorial manner that meant nothing; he had been very good at making money, and very good at picking clients. Yet he was also known for his love of good writing. From the little we talked, I think this was true; he loved Nabokov, as did I, and I was desperate to believe in him. I sent him my book to see if he liked it, and he said he thought it 'remarkable'. He read it on some Greek island and left a praising message on my answerphone. What a fool I was; I kept the tape for weeks.

I went to see the first, and much more simpatico, agent who thought he had inherited me. He sat in his office with my book on his lap, and I saw he did like it, and was slightly hurt when I told him I was probably going to leave, though he had a wealth of clients, and of course soon got over it (why was I so stupid? I liked this first man, instinctively trusted him, could talk to him, yet I opted for the austere unknown because I thought he could magically lift me into the literary stratosphere, with his other clients. I thought I was making the right decision, yet lunch with this second man was empty and uncomfortable, and part of me wondered if his reputation came partly from his height, and his upper-class drawl, for literary agents are not usually so lofty. I should have listened to my animal instincts rather than the vaulting ambition of my brain.)

Thus bolstered by the good opinions of two agents who had to praise me to represent me – which does not mean they were insincere, but an agent's job is to hook new names – and my husband's enthusiasm (he read the book with the doors open on our green garden, as spring came on; he loved me, he loved it, but warm April possibly hazed his senses) – I dispatched the book to HarperCollins. I was mostly buoyant. Now everything would change.

Yet part of me was anxious. Such a very long novel. It was partly to do with the look of the manuscript. It's part of the 'frame' that, according to psychologists, conditions the greater part of people's response; what they know, or think they know, before they start reading. *The Keeper of the Gate* was the first book I had written straight on to computer (*Where are the Snows* and *Lost Children* were both drafted longhand). I used a huge font (why?),14 pt, too many spaces, too many ellipses. In manuscript this novel ran to nearly 500 pages. Perhaps I was unconsciously trying to say to the publishing world, 'This is big, this is a substantial book.' Probably it just looked long and shapeless.

My relationship with the new editor at HarperCollins Flamingo was non-existent, so the ground my work fell on was unprepared (*always get on with your editor*. Sometimes you really do need advice.) He had suggested we meet for a drink at intervals to discuss progress. But I never discussed my works-in-progress. Besides, at first there *was* no progress: not until the first four months of 1994 did the novel suddenly burst free of chaos. And this book was, to say the least of it, unusual. Not the manuscript to send to the new editor who, it's cruel to say, but true, was best known for having commissioned a novel inspired by a TV coffee advert.

Why was my sixth novel unusual? Because it was about race. The germ of it was a racial killing. In April 1993, the black student Stephen Lawrence had been murdered at a bus-stop in south-east London by racist white youths. It was a horrible case, one of the sudden outbreaks of savagery that tells us London isn't just a great city of endlessly mixing genes and peoples. We were not post-racist, then or now; we merely legislate against it, and rub along together, and marry each other, and hope for the best, which mostly happens – but every so often, so does the worst.

My personal experience of the crime sounds trivial. Rosa's school was in Brent, which had, at the time, the highest proportion of black people in the UK. Naturally Rosa had black friends, naturally I was friends with their mothers, Rochelle's mother, Shakira's mother, a friendship built on shared love of our children. But British black people felt burning indignation over this murder. One of their best, a good student, a boy who should have become a lawyer, had been senselessly killed by white racists. The veil was lifted; their worst fears were true. For a while, all white people stood accused. And I found that my black friends, who I liked and valued, for a while were unable to meet my eyes. A veil had come down, though it didn't last.

But I still felt accountable. What had I actually done to dissociate myself from the murderers? In 1982, when American Cruise missiles were about to be sent to Britain, I had written my anti-war novel *The Burning Book*; in 1988, the murder of eighty-four-year-old anti-nuclear campaigner Hilda Murrell had inspired my fourth novel, *Grace*. What was I going to do this time?

I wanted to protest; as Dickens did against the evils of his day, and Thackeray, and George Eliot – so many great nineteenth-century novelists. It didn't make them less literary. Many of my literary models are modernist – Virginia Woolf, Vladimir Nabokov – but for me the modernist aesthetic breaks down when it isolates the writer from the world. Like the modernists, I love pattern, and try to give each book an overall controlling form, but I also have one eye on reality. I want my books to express the whole of me, politics and jokes as well as love of beauty.

What kind of country, what kind of family, might produce racists like the five white thugs? This was what I needed to write about. What did it say about my city? For I had become a Londoner, and Stephen Lawrence was one of our own. But so were the thugs, the murderers.

In Kensal Rise, the subject was everywhere. I heard the things said by the white workmen who came to the flat; they weren't middle-class, and hadn't learned to hide it. They seemed to particularly hate Indians, who they were afraid were after their jobs, but they didn't like Africans and Caribbeans either. The reasons were many: 'they don't pay'; 'you can't trust them'. Yet for the first time in my life I was living in a world where there were equal numbers of black and white, which in many ways stifled prejudice, for it was simply too tiring to keep noticing colour; there were many families with biracial children, often strikingly beautiful, especially when young, with wild blonde curls and deep cupid's-bow lips, a new perfection born from difference. Clearly, in many cases, all around me sex and love were overcoming prejudice. But in other ways, there were still two parallel worlds. I saw how people tended not to see one another. How white people turned to white people to ask for directions, or information, and vice versa. How black people looked surprised to be talked to. As a person and as a novelist, it was impossible not to notice (I think we have come some way since then.) Then I made a friend, Hanna Sakyi, who rapidly became important to me. It began as a convenience relationship, for she started an after-school club at Rosa's school, but I quickly saw how special Hanna was. Rosa loved her at once, and still does. She was Ghanaian, and very black, but then, everything about Hanna was 'very'. She was very funny, and very sharp, and had a laugh that rolled around a room, and strong self-possession, a sense of herself that made people sit up and take notice; she was very big, and very beautiful, with soulful dark eyes, high cheekbones, dimples, full lips, a short curving upper lip that made her look youthful, and small snowy teeth with a kissing gap. She came to tea, she came to supper. We began talking, and never stopped. At first the one thing we didn't mention was that she was black and I was white. These taboos are strong, and our fears are great. Then one day we started talking about it, and talked about it, for a while, a lot; after which we got over it, mostly forgot it, and went on with being friends as normal. When Rosa was baptised, aged ten, Hanna was one of her three godmothers, and Nick and I are godparents to her son Robbie. I have other black friends, some of them writers, but Hanna gave me courage to write the book.

I wanted to write about the Britain I loved, my sense of which stretched back to the '50s. It was my parents' country too, the place their generation had fought for in the war, the country my great-uncles had died for. They believed they had risked everything so life would be better, with a new, fairer deal for everyone. The Gees were Labour through and through, and the ideals I grew up with were co-operative, communal, although my father himself, of course, like his father, like so many old Labour patriarchs, was fiercely individualistic and territorial. My father, the bane and the lodestar of my life, who made me a member of the awkward squad, rebelling against him and everything else ...

My aim was to write about a racial murder, yet I was being drawn back into confronting my father, without my knowledge, against my will. I started to create a character.

This was Alfred White, the park keeper, who ran his fiefdom for the public good, just as Dad believed in his job as a head teacher. I didn't see Alfred was a version of my father, but looking back, it should have been obvious. Side by side with Alfred was his wife, May White, to whom I gave the name of my mother's mother, who loved reading, as my own mother did, who wrote poems and had a secret life, like her, and whose favourite book was a copy of Tennyson that Mum had been given as a form prize. The actual copy! And she loved and feared Alfred, and hid things from her husband, as my mother did. And yet, in my head, I wasn't actually writing about my parents, because if I had consciously told myself that, I would have drawn back, afraid. And so, in the shelter of a cloud of unknowing, I began to write my way into the book.

Alfred's park was modelled on beautiful Roundwood Park, my local park, founded in 1900, with its stone sundial and drinking fountain, aviary and flower-beds, its little café, its plane-trees, its roses, its shady lawns where conversation murmured, its gentle hill overlooking the graveyard. But it was also a metaphor for Britain, the country where Stephen Lawrence had been killed. And slowly the book started to come together.

Alfred White had three children (as did my father). Like us, there were two brothers and a sister: Darren, Shirley, and poor little Dirk.

Though there the resemblances really did end, for there was not a jot of likeness to my brothers; neither of them is ignorant, a racist, or cheesily in love with America, like Darren, and though I'd love to look sexy and creamy like Shirley – maybe I am sexy and creamy inside? – I am thin and wiry and always in a hurry. Yet in some way that afterwards I couldn't deny, Alfred was my father, and May my mother, and the book was my way of forgiving my father, for in the end Alfred would be tested, and my father had never been short of moral courage.

A brief sketch of the plot: there's a row in the park. A black family has walked on the grass, Alfred remonstrates and is accused of racism, becomes enraged and falls down with a stroke. The family gather round his bedside. Rich, shallow Darren, a journalist, comes back from the States to join Shirley and Dirk. Shirley is the widow of a Ghanaian academic, Kojo. Dirk, the youngest and dimmest child, hates black people partly because he has grown up bathed in his father's mild, old-fashioned racism, but more actively and jealously because his sister married Kojo. Dirk works in the failing local paper-shop, and when an Indian businessman takes it over, his hatred and frustration boil over into murder. And the parents find out. What is to be done?

It was the question the whole country was trying to answer. The police investigation into Stephen Lawrence's death was scandalously poor. Though an inquest would eventually give a verdict of unlawful killing by five named youths, no one was ever convicted or punished. Something had gone terribly wrong in Britain, not just the murder but the way we dealt with it. When the report of the McPherson Inquiry came out, in 1999, the police were found guilty of something new, 'institutional racism', and everyone was forced to look at themselves and their own institutions, and ask hard questions. We began to see racism everywhere.

But I was too early for that changed climate. Many things in my novel must have been shocking. Dirk's racism was explicit and detailed, and I told it from inside his consciousness, a technique I also used for his father's more mundane racism. (I did distance the novel's moral viewpoint from Dirk's by making him ignorant, in many ways an idiot. His impoverished vocabulary and imagination make his account of the world comic and pathetic. The comedy may have been the hardest thing; some people were too shocked to laugh at him, although my black friends did find him funny.) Black people's experience of white racism was also shown at length on the page. The book made uncomfortable reading for anyone, but maybe especially for those white liberals who thought that racism was in the past.

I submitted my manuscript in 1995. After a long pause, HarperCollins turned it down.

They turned it down! I could not believe it. I was Maggie Gee, on my sixth novel, my career could surely only go upwards. I would choose my agent and my publisher ... but no, *the publisher had turned me down*. Nick took me to Wales. A deep, terrible pain only slowly ebbed as we sat on the sand. By the fourth day I was human again. But an accident had happened, a brutal car-crash. *Obviously someone else would jump at the book, but still, HarperCollins had turned me down.* (Could I be plucked out of my new glossy world of literary success so easily? I had heard of other well-known authors being rejected, and had always thought, 'They must have written a bad book.' But now the same thing had happened to me.)

If you had told me then what I slowly learned, over the next twelve months of grim education – that my book would be turned down by almost every mainstream literary publisher in London – I do not believe I could have taken it in. It would have been unthinkable.

I have already confessed I was not careful enough. The book was a little windy and baggy. It needed a good hard edit, another three months of thought and work. Yes, I was also unwise in my tactics, expecting to change agents and publishers at random. I am trying to give weight to the many factors that contributed to my book becoming homeless, for I do believe that, as with homeless people, the problem was too many factors colliding. But I still come to this conclusion: the novel was turned down partly, perhaps mainly, because the subject was unacceptable. Britain didn't want to think about racism. It wasn't ready, though one day it would be. In 1995, publishers turned their backs.

The rejection letters were curious. Too long, too insulting or self-justifying, some just inappropriate: one editor remarked that she 'simply disagreed', though generally you don't disagree with a novel. Many of them used the same adjectives; 'dark' was a favourite, which should have been amusing. I put them, one by one, in a file under the desk, and after a few, I wrote 'DISASTER' on the cover. As with one miscarriage, you become more prone to fearfully anticipate a second. I was more afraid each time the new agent sent it out, but still I took each letter as a blow to the heart, unwilling to believe it, raging, protesting. (Poor Nick. He could not have been more tested. But he took it all. He was my rock.)

And, as I already mentioned, a kindly acquaintance, Di Marcus, to whom I will always be grateful, said, 'This is when character tells.' My friends: how much they have taught me and helped me. But I wasn't so sure that my character would help me. I felt weak, angry, fatally wounded.

What resources did I have that helped me to survive? My husband, Rosa, and the self-belief my parents gave me when I was a child. Nick never faltered; he continued to say, 'This is your best book. I believe in it.' In the end I turned on him, furious. 'You're deluded. It's your fault, you should have told me it was hopeless. They can't all be wrong, surely, can they?' Stubbornly he kept on insisting they were wrong.

The immediate worries were financial. I had expected a payment of £35,000, the balance owing on my contract, and had run into debt in anticipation, though I hated debt, because of my background. I had a contract; the money must arrive. It didn't arrive. My overdraft grew. For a year, the agent kept sending the book out. Drip by drip, confidence and hope were eroded.

Some money arrived in dribs and drabs. The first, kind and gentlemanly, agent, the one I should have stayed with, together with Mark Le Fanu of the Society of Authors, leaned on HarperCollins to give me a token pay-off of £5,000. (Later on in the whole protracted saga, the Society of Authors gave me a grant of £3,000 to get me back on my feet again. We authors need our organisations, which line up behind us in hard times; not just the Society of Authors, but Public Lending Right, the stalwart body that collects money from the government whenever people borrow our books from libraries, and ALCS, which protects our copyrights and sends us money we never knew we'd earned. Young writers, join up and support these allies! When you need them, they will be there for you.)

Then an opportune phone call came from Penny Smith, a lecturer at Northumbria University in Newcastle, who liked my work, and taught my novel *Grace*, inviting me to do a three-month residency up there, two days a week, and despite the travelling, I jumped at it. My friend Barbara lent me £5,000 which at least plugged the hole I had opened up. Neither of us knew it would take me seven or eight years to pay back. And as the year turned, and the rejections kept coming, I began reviewing for my bread and butter. That most painstaking and generous literary editor, John Coldstream at the *Daily Telegraph*, perhaps getting wind that I was in trouble, started asking me to review regularly: once a month, then twice a month, then almost every week. Without it I couldn't have paid my share of the mortgage. It kept me alive, and my name in the papers. But my ego was shrivelling, all the same. Everything had changed. Perhaps I was ... finished.

Depression overwhelmed me; I felt I was drowning. Instead I made myself get up every day and go swimming at the Willesden Sports Centre just down the road, in the very early morning, so that by the time I came home to the emptiness, something good at least had happened, one good thing a day, however small. There was blood in my cheeks, and breath in my body, and the glow that comes with having exercised. My mind and its ambitions had led me astray; my body, recovering its strength, saved me. I put my trust in it, my animal body. I was swimming more lengths: fifty, eighty. *I was my father's daughter. I would go on.*

I asked writers of colour to read the novel. I feared they would hate it, like everyone else, but to them, of course, the racism I wrote about was not unbelievable, nor even remarkable, it was just part of the substance of their days. I was given much-needed encouragement by the novelist Mike Phillips, then writer-in-residence at the South Bank, by Bernardine Evaristo, author of *The Emperor's Babe* and *Blonde Roots*, and by Colin Grant, Marcus Garvey's biographer. I will never forget their kindness, for their own paths as writers were not entirely easy, but they all took the time to read that long novel, in manuscript, closely and critically, and sent me with advice and a blessing on my way. I needed their critique, but even more, their blessing. It was all I had to keep the show on the road.

But I still felt terrible shame and unease when other people asked about my writing. I was unable to admit I had been rejected. Yet my internal landscape was slowly shifting. I *had* been rejected. So what would I do now? The tall agent was becoming more languid, and talked, one day when I went to see him, about another author, very well-known, who had written a book that was turned down. 'He decided in the end he had to let it go.' The lesson was indirect, but clear enough. Time had slipped on. We were heading fast for 1997, and I hadn't had a book out since 1994.

Down the road from us a couple, Steve and Suzanne, had moved in with a daughter, Isobel, two years younger than Rosa, and the man, Steve Shill, was a writer and director who later migrated to America and worked on *The Sopranos* and *The Wire*. As usual, new friends brought new ideas. (*Never just stay at home and suffer.*) Steve lent me a guide to film structure. At the same time, John Coldstream sent me a book to review called *The Next 500 Years*, by Adrian Berry, an overview of scientific predictions. It was speculative, but fizzed with ideas. The piece of information that excited me most was that, contrary to what I had always assumed, our temperate climate was not the norm; in fact, the earth's default state was ice. Ice ages lasted for 100,000 years; arrived suddenly, over ten or twenty years; and were interspersed by temperate periods of only 8,000–14,000 years. And it was 12,000 years since the last ice age. The maths were suggestive. My mind started spinning.

With both books in my bag I travelled up to Newcastle to do a session with the creative writing students on 'Structure'. Structure is the weakness of creative writing courses; only brief pieces of writing can be discussed in a two-hour workshop, so some students become brilliant at writing individual chapters of novels, but have a weak overall grasp of structure or story. (And too many twentieth-century novels are weak on story. Yet story is what readers like, and they're right, it's what we need from art: stories to help us navigate the confusion of our own life-stories.) I read Steve's book on film structure on the train, and liked its vigour. Yes, three acts, like every good drama. With plot points and a mid-point, a swoop up to the climax, a dip to the end – I loved this stuff. I sat on the train and redrafted this structure in terms of a 250-page novel. On which page should the plot points come? And the climax? I made a diagram for the students, and suggested that they try it out.

On the three-hour journey home, things crystallised. I was a writer, but what was I writing? It was time to write myself out of trouble. The only thing I could do was write, and no one, *no one* could stop me writing (*Vic's daughter would never give up*). The two books in my bag, and the students, came together. I took my own advice, and tried it out. I roughed out a story, with three acts, and plot points. We were in the middle of the next century, and an ice age had come upon us very fast. And I remember the excitement of sitting down at home and working into the night on the outline of a story as I followed, scene by scene, my model film structure. I had needed an idea, something utterly different from the rambling themes of the earlier novel; I needed a rope to guide me to the end, for I would not have dared follow my nose again, after my big, loose structure had led me to disaster. Within two days, I was given both things. I took what I was given and ran with it.

I wrote *The Ice People* in less than six months. I wrote it as comedy, as satire, though there were links with *The Keeper of the Gate*: I had a biracial hero, Saul, who was trying to take his son Luke back to Africa, away from the ice that was advancing from the north. The arrow of population flow was reversed. It was Africa's turn to restrict immigration. This new book was clear and short, with plenty of adventure. It felt totally different from its predecessor. My spirits improved. I was doing what I did. Now life would surely revert to normal. Nick loved the book. I sent it to the agent. He was less expressive, but said it was 'good'. He sent it to our joint first choice of publishers – and of course there were fewer to send to than before, not just because the publishing world was contracting as more independents were sucked into conglomerates, but because I had been published by several already.

My hopes were high, but it began again, the catalogue of disappointing letters, and this time it was even harder to bear. I couldn't believe it, but it reran, the disaster movie of rejection. (Yet I knew they were wrong. This time they were wrong. I was absolutely sure this book was good. The other one had been so strange and unwieldy that I could hardly bear to think about it, but this one was carefully edited. I was over the worst of my RSI and the chaotic haste of Rosa's early childhood. I do have a cool side; I am hard on myself, but my considered opinion was, this book hacked it.)

Where to go next? I could not give up. I had put the first book aside to drain, but I could not do that with a second. I went for another discussion with the agent. I could see the tall man was wearying of me, but I didn't want to acknowledge it, because if he gave up on me, I had lost the lot: publisher, book, this man who gave me status. But status, between writer and agent, is a two-way thing. I had not considered how it affected him, this wry, reserved man who liked to win, representing a writer who was being turned down. I should have paid attention to something he said after a rejection letter that was particularly offensive: 'Yes ... probably aimed at me, not you.' I did hear something he said that was so terrible I had to hive it off into a part of my brain where I could bear to hear it later. He had a drawling, smiling manner which had become vaguer and less intimate. He still had few words, but these words cut. 'I wouldn't say that in the present state of the market it's a book that *demands* to be published.' We were nearing the end of our barren story, but I had to hang on. I had nowhere else to go.

The end came after a rejection from the last big publisher on our list. I wrote the agent a short, polite letter asking him to send the manuscript to two small independent publishers, Serpent's Tail and Richard Cohen Books. But the tall man did not deal with small independents. They were too short, they were under his radar. He didn't say this, but I would hypothesise two reasons. One, they pay less. He was a businessman. Of course agents deal with small independents, but in our case there was no real warmth or liking to make up for the missing money. Second, and perhaps more important: if I was going to be turned down by publishers he thought of as so lowly ... he would be turned down by them too. This was simply unacceptable.

He ended the relationship between us by fax, which arrived at the end of an afternoon. It came scrolling smudgily into my house where Nick and Rosa had to live too, where either of them might have read it first. I suppose he was afraid to speak to me. I wish

I could remember what he said, but it was just something coolly neutral: 'I don't deal with those particular publishers ... better if we no longer represent you.'

I know there was no malice behind it. I know that for him it was just business, and I was no longer a business proposition. I had fooled myself into thinking it was more – some agents are doggedly loyal to their authors – but no, I had deceived myself. Beware, young writers. Agents need to make money.

That was the nadir. That was the worst. You may wonder, reader, where this chapter is going as I drag you with me down this long mudslide, but take heart, for this was the turning point. It was Nick who told me this, for when I came through clutching the cheap, cowardly paper I had ripped from the mouth of the grey machine, his antic self, his adorable self that cannot be repressed or changed, shouted, 'HURRAY! Hurray, hurray! Thank God, at last you are rid of that ——. Now everything will get better, Magsie.' At the time I thought he was utterly mad, though I loved him for it more than I can say, but it was true, my fate was back in our hands.

I sent off the manuscripts to the two publishers I had chosen. Richard Cohen Books was an interesting one; Richard had been a famous editor at Hodder, credited (falsely) with rewriting Jeffrey Archer; but he really had edited countless high-profile literary authors and books, Fay Weldon's scintillating *Puffball* among them. He had left Hodder to found his own firm. It was small, but his reputation gave it status.

A preliminary letter came back at once, from Richard himself, acknowledging receipt, but also, in a humorous way that fell on my bruised ego like irony, saying something like 'but why would such a famous author be sending to a little outfit like ours?' Naturally I did not send a ten-page answer.

Even that slight contact made me hope, though I had hoped too much, and had too many knock-backs. Yet a small voice inside me said, 'This *has* to work, because if not, this time I can't bear it.'

Then I remembered what you had to do when life was too much for you to bear. It was the week after I had sent the books off. Nick had gone to work, and Rosa to school. I was alone; the house was sunny. Hope swirled up into that glory of sunlight and with it, the terror of absolute despair. Before I knew what I was doing, I was down on my knees, on the comfortless jute flooring, praying, my forehead cupped in my hands, the knuckles pressed into the ridges of jute. The sunlight blazed above my head. 'Please God please God, may I get a phone call. I just can't bear this any more.' Red basket-weave marks on my hands, my knees.

And the phone rang. It was Richard Cohen. I could hear the smile in his voice. He had read my book, liked it, admired it. Yes, they were very keen to publish. They weren't rich though. Would £5,000 be enough?

Like all the best film scripts, it wasn't quite over at the moment when the hero arrived to save me. But Richard did have a heroic mien: he was tall and craggy, an Olympic fencer still, in his fifties, with a baritone voice and a head of curls. He introduced me to Christine Casley, the wonderful editor who would go on to edit my next three books (*my next three books*. That casual phrase that for two years I'd been unable to take for granted.) I liked everyone in that small firm with their offices off Soho Square. It felt like old-fashioned publishing. They got on with each other, they believed in all the books. It was a happiness to go in and see them, to use, again, with infinitely more pleasure, the innocent phrase 'my publisher', to descend from the square to that bright, bookish basement.

But financially, the wolves were slinking round the door, clattering the lids of the dustbins outside. Richard had sunk his inheritance into the firm, but he was an editor, not an accountant. I had grown more steely through those three hard years, and I remember one day how I went down the steps to see this tall man who had done so much for me, determined to get the second half of my advance, payable on delivery, now I had given him the edited text. He had great charm, and we liked each other. He did not refuse, but said something like, 'We don't have to do it now, do we? I could put it in the post.' All the conventions of politeness said, 'Oh, put it in the post, Richard.' But the steel in me said, 'Now would be great.' I left the office, his cheque hot in my hand, and paid it in to the bank with indecent haste.

Publication was scheduled for some time in autumn. The cover proof shimmered, a cave of blue ice. Christine Casley's editing had cured me for ever of my overuse of ellipses and italics. We had a summer holiday in Cornwall with Rosa and her friend Aline, camping near a surfing beach. It was a brilliant holiday, a treat for the body, walking on rolling cliffs and long sands, lying on our backs to watch shooting stars. I was very happy that things had got better, infinitely grateful for ordinariness. The girls were twelve and fourteen: a lovely age. They stayed in bed in their tent in the morning while Nick and I had time on our own. I was supposed to ring Richard from a callbox – this was before the days of mobiles – to check the last few corrections to the text and get a definite publication date. I remember I left the girls and Nick on the beach at St Ives, below the new Tate. I had to walk through some cavernous, hellish entertainment place to find the callbox. *Going back into the underworld.*

Richard was sounding slightly evasive. Various things were going on, he said. He had a few 'troubles'. He was wondering ... perhaps it would be better to publish in the spring? Then he could really make a good job of it. There would be more money, he'd be on a firmer footing. I was caught off guard, and did not disagree.

I went back to the beach. The girls were playing, the sand was white, it was the same as before, but a terrible dread began to crystallise as I relayed this apparently anodyne message.

Nick's reaction was instinctive and immediate. He went through his pockets to find more coins. 'You go back and tell him he's got to publish. It has to be now, Mags, you've got to get it out. And if he's short of money, we'll find it somehow. I'll find it. I will. Go and tell him that.' I trusted Nick's instincts. I was impressed. I went back through hell to talk to Richard.

He did find the money. They made a lovely book, with expensive paper and a cover of austere cobalt beauty, an ice-cave leading away into light, something silver, mysterious, just around the corner. Twelve copies arrived: I held the first in my hands, electric with joy. I was alive again. I have never loved a book so much as *The Ice People*, that cool blue drink after three years of drought. Now at last I realised how precious books were, how hard and risky it was to write them, how chancy the business of jumping through the hoops.

But I had made it in the nick of time. On the day the book was published, the publisher went bust. The launch party for my book was a wake. Half the literary world had turned up, not just for me but out of sympathy for Richard. We must have sold sixty or seventy books that evening, because I caught a muttered conversation between two of the staff as they totted up the takings: 'Over £600. That'll pay X's wages.' The reviews of this book that the tall, superior agent had said 'did not *demand* to be published' were almost uniformly ecstatic. Jeremy Paxman invited me on 'Start the Week' and was intelligent and enthusiastic, saying I was 'up there with Orwell and Huxley'; Eric Korn praised me highly in the *TLS*; George Melly raved in the *Telegraph*; Fay Weldon applauded in the *Literary Review*: as in a happy dream, everybody loved it. *The Times*, *Time Out*, all fell into line.

The best of Richard's list was bought up by another small publisher, Metro, run by the impressive Suzanne McDadd who, after my time there, had been a director of Faber and Faber. She stayed up half the night reading *The Ice People*, loved it, and paid me for the paperback rights. Soon they were preparing a mass market paperback, its jacket lavishly decked with quotes. The *Mail on Sunday* book club made it their book of the week: Rose Tremain wrote a praising feature to accompany the *Mail* offer. Richard Cohen told me Metro sold 30,000 copies. And now the story almost dips into farce, for Metro Books, in turn, went bankrupt, and I never did get my royalties.

But the book itself has continued to be successful. It is now in its third edition, the most recent described by the *Observer* as 'masterly ... one of the first great novels of the globally warmed world'. Last year my new agent sold the television rights.

I picked up the threads of my career. I started on what was once unthinkable: rereading, and revising, *The Keeper of the Gate*, which for years I'd been unable to bear to look at. And I saw Nick had a point. There was something there. In fact, perhaps ... could he even be right? Was it possible that actually it was my best book?

And now I come to the nub of this chapter, the point I want to make with this long story of the worst five years of my professional life, a story I don't enjoy retelling because I have to re-experience the terror of failing. Many novelists stall at a certain point. Their profession deserts them. They are no longer wanted. And I was so nearly one of them.

What I learned was, there's little logic in this world. No team of angels combing the wind to see that no one good slips through. No internal aesthetic, no guarantee. Literary history is not foolproof, no more than art history is. I realised this long ago, when I first started travelling and visiting the local galleries wherever I went, in Dusseldorf, Salzburg, Berne, Bournemouth: that art history is an approximation. I always found at least one or two painters I had never heard of, but thought remarkable. Perhaps they didn't paint enough; perhaps they lived in the wrong place, or were ahead of their time, or knew the wrong people, or didn't live long enough, or weren't pushy enough. Somehow they slipped off the historical map where the path of the famous is crudely marked out. (I see the same phenomenon on courses I teach. It's not always the most talented ones who go on to be successful; it's the luckiest and most determined.) I started to put my observations of the literary world together with my reading on evolutionary biology; life was struggle, and all human activities related to our jostling for advantage. Were the other things just illusory, then, the watchwords I'd lived by, truth, beauty?

I saw that literature had never been the self-sufficient world the modernists tried to make for themselves. They did it, in fact, by self-publishing, by patronage. They also built cliques who believed (or believed they believed) that only beauty mattered; in fact they were cohorts who pushed each other through. Virginia and Leonard Woolf showed sound common sense by founding their own publishing firm. The Hogarth Press liberated them from being dependent on commercial whim, which Virginia was too fragile to survive, but they ran it as professionals, and made money.

What was writing, at bottom, biologically? A human activity, like painting and sculpting, a skill we use to make a reputation in our group. These skills aren't magic; they come from a connection between senses, dreaming brain, and hand (in earlier times, when narratives were oral, between brain, voice and performing body). Storytellers always had value to the tribe, because humans like novelty, and laughter, the pleasure of adventure, of happy endings, of listening to ancestral memories or sometimes experiencing sorrow safely.

Once we could measure our value at the fireside. The link between story and body was close, and storytellers were close to their audience. But twenty-first-century stories are encoded in books, which are products. The audience aimed for must be ever larger, because the middlemen, publishers, want to make money. Not that they really know what will sell; they are gamblers, the gurus of sales and marketing to whom commissioning editors defer, but all the same, it's hard to get past them. There is no direct interface where ordinary readers can gauge our skill at storytelling, where we can find and meet our audience – just the vast faceless spaces of the net, where all of us are equally lost.

I saw how late capitalism was transforming the book trade. As the giant firms sucked up the independents, they aimed to sell more copies of fewer books. Easier for them to expend effort on a small range of easy-to-sell products. The logic of copying, of repetition. The technologies of advertising and mass reproduction have grown lethally effective since Walter Benjamin. The more a name is heard or copied, the more, subliminally, people think it's the best. The logic of it all was leading big publishers away from writers and towards celebrities. It cost no money to promote the already-famous; they advertise themselves, by falling out of clubs. Thence the tyranny of the big book chains and their charts, overrun by celebrity novels and autobiographies. Perfectly respected and serious publishers talked proudly about 'the death of the mid-list', to show they too were out there, swimming with sharks; but really they were just making sad boasts about the loss of variety and interest.

(I was simplifying, but the chill I felt could not be dispersed by my own morning swim.)

But couldn't we fall back on our critical gatekeepers, the literary editors, the reviewers? Would quality be saved by the books pages?

I knew there were good critics and valiant editors. I had often been kindly treated by both. Yet what I saw – what I still see now – is in fact a world of progressive illusions, where adjectives build upon one another. A writer is praised, and wins a big prize: a quantum leap in his career has happened. The praise will now increase, and there will be more prizes. Soon he will be 'a great writer' (when I look at my own generation, the 'great' are mostly men, and I say this as a woman who reads and admires both genders). Partly it's the psychological effect I have mentioned, where people judge in the light of their prior expectations. The 'frame' is all-important to what we think we see. Yet if you try to lay aside the frame, and look hard at the work, book by book, there may have been no improvement at all. If anything, there has been a falling off. But we have to believe, because others do. Conformism is a safe stratagem. That (truly great) genius Hans Andersen said it all in his story, 'The Emperor's New Clothes', where no one had the courage to break the illusion that the emperor had a splendid new set of garments (in fact he was naked, had been conned by flash tailors who told him they were using a magical new cloth, but it took a small child to believe his own eyes and tell the truth, that the emperor had no clothes – all the adults in the crowd were in thrall to consensus).

Critics like their towers, their increments, their sense that they are watching a success story, that their own praise can add to it. It becomes taken for granted that certain names are landmarks, and the more they are repeated, the more it seems true, for they start to come easily to everybody's lips. Once again, the power of repetition; the relief of simplifying a landscape. But it doesn't prove they're good. They are merely successful.

I saw it as a jungle, from that time on, where there were few disinterested observers. That's what we need, since there are no literary angels; we want teams of skilled taxonomists, Nabokovian naturalists, protected like jurors from prevailing opinions, ideal readers who sift slowly and carefully and add to knowledge with what they tell us. That's not what we get. We get reviewers, rushing too fast to earn their pittance, trying to be funny or shocking or rude or do anything that will get them noticed. They write for themselves, not to describe the books. Often they are writing *about* themselves. They don't see what they do as a service to literature; it's journalism; the books are fodder. It was a sinister, irrevocable step when the names of reviewers first became larger than the names of the authors they were writing about. (But reviewers also have to make their names. They are struggling too. Why should I expect them to be different?

We are all out for our evolutionary advantage.) And the critics' own position is no longer secure, for the arts pages in the newspapers are shrinking, the literary editors are being sacked, the newspapers themselves are fleeing to the net because the young no longer buy the physical papers.

So what are writers, in this jungle? I wondered. (I meant, when we were not at home writing, that private, low-key act, the core of it all, which I was forgetting in my cynical inventory. The writing, which can't be faked, or stage-managed, unless you're a celeb and pay someone else to do it. The work, the work, I had to cling on to that, for the world I was seeing was very bleak.)

In the jungle, writers are opportunists. We are show-offs, trying to display our coats. We need to be the most beautiful and youthful, we need to have novelty, we need to have mates: a pack or a cohort to shoulder us through, to rush us on upwards through the trees. If we fall, we must be sure to get up quickly, for if we lie there, bleeding, we will die down there. And we, too, are here for our own advantage, struggling for the light of fame or money, for we, too, have to pay the bills, we, too, have young to bring up, and set on their own path to evolutionary advantage.

(Yet there was something else: it was about the work. *All about the work*. I would return to that.)

Of course, some good writers do well in the jungle. Of course, reviewers sometimes get it right. But it isn't inevitable; it isn't even normal. If you want to know where the best writers are, you can't tell by reading the literary pages, or going to big bookshops, or looking at prize lists. You must read for yourself, and think for yourself, or listen to voices you know and trust: private readers: truth-tellers.

I still think most of that analysis is true. And yet it left out a lot of 'human nature', it left out the joy and pleasure people get when they find something they genuinely like, and publishers, booksellers, critics are people; it left out the fact that, alongside the conformism that biologists tell us serves most people well (which direction do you run in when a flood is coming? No time to think, just follow the others), there are always people who like to be different, who are sceptical and original. Independent publishers like Saqi and Telegram, Profile and Tindal Street Press, Salt and Comma; independent booksellers like Foyles or John Sandoe's or my locals, Willesden Books, Kilburn Books, the Queen's Park Bookshop.

And then there is the work. Come back to that. Get up on the wire, walk the line in the sunlight. Breathe, concentrate, find the nerve. What is it about? Something says '*my soul*', and I am uneasy, and turn away, embarrassed. My being-in-the-world expressed as performance. The rhythm of my body imprinting on the page, what my eyes have seen, what my heart has lived. And the movement of my hand lets me share it with others. I am here, now. I am writing the truth of it. For most writers, work is not just a product.

My book had fallen foul of the market, but rereading it, I believed in it. The question was, where could I go? How could I get my portrait of Britain out to the British?

Once again, friends of mine stepped in, Moris Farhi, the Turkish writer, campaigner and intellectual, and his wife (and editor) Nina Farhi. Nina: it is still hard to write about her, those intelligent brown eyes and bird-like profile under a Greek girl's thicket of curls: with whom I would talk passionately about novels while Moris ('Musa') cooked succulent chicken, his deep voice interjecting knowledge from the stove. Nina: who played football with us in the garden, lithe and laughing but a deadly opponent. We discussed Fay Weldon and Anita Brookner and our beloved only daughters, and our central theme was often writing, though Nina was a well-known psychoanalyst (she died, alas, most fierce and beautiful and missed, her mind still the mind of an eagle, a claw-

Moris and Nina with Rosa – Nina once saved Rosa from falling downstairs with a magnificent goal-keeper's dive

hold on life as the sky went dark, while I was finishing this book. How can such presence become an absence?)

Nina and Moris both loved *The White Family* and discussed gravely what to do about it. Moris showed the book to his friend and publisher, the Lebanese sculptor and writer Mai Ghoussoub, co-founder with André Gaspard of Saqi, which had been in existence for over twenty years. I am sure Moris encouraged her in certain expectations; probably he told her it was wonderful; in other words, the 'frame' was right.

She read it expecting it to be good because she loved and trusted Moris. I knew she had the manuscript. I dared not hope.

Only my diary can truly tell the story of those unforgettable three days in late April.

Tuesday April 17 2001 was just an 'ordinary' day. My daughter was 'grumpy', I went on trying to write 'a new book' (it was the start of *The Flood*, in fact), but the diary says 'a mere 650 words so far'. Then the page breaks into big, bold, type:

> Oh happiness, oh unimaginable happiness that may yet turn into absolute bliss, for this afternoon … the phone rang, and it was a melodious woman's voice, foreign. I stood in the grubby hall and took it in. 'Mai … Mai Ghoussoub … We have a friend in common, Moris Farhi … I have phoned to tell you I have finished

reading your book, and I have enjoyed it very much ...
It was such a pleasure. It is literature. Literature does
not judge ... All your characters are human. And the
end. I liked it very much, the end. Because it moves
it outside of London and makes it universal ... Very
touching. I think I enjoyed it more than any manuscript
I have read in a long time ...'

Then there was apparently a note of caution, for she said the book
would be discussed at a meeting they would have over the next day
or so, and her last words were disquieting: 'I hope we meet, at any
rate.'

Once I had put the phone down, though, I was 'suffused and
energised with hope ... someone likes my White Elephant!'

Wednesday April 18

Still fizzing. I wrote a little more on the new novel,
diary, fun with Rosa – but the weather is cold – 'It's
winter again,' said Nick. No phone call from Saqi yet
at 5 pm.

Thursday April 19

What a day. Fear started to replace joy some time
around the end of the morning, Nothing could protect
me from gloom ... as the afternoon went on in the
empty house. Had Mai's meeting been on Wednesday?
Had it been this morning? No call meant bad news. I
hate the feeling that I can do nothing, nothing to help
myself – not my busybodying nature to do nothing and
accept what comes.

I tried to read and got – next to nowhere. Nick
rang [from the BBC] around four – any news? No.

He was full of love. 'Go and read outside,' he said –
then, 'Maybe not, it's raining.'

Actually I did go outside and read, in the garden, on
the step, though it was splashing with April rain which
dimpled my pages, and there was April sun, too. Wild
violets where the grass had given up. Magnolias in the
next-door garden. I thought, 'I mind terribly about this,
I've just been kidding myself that I would understand
if Saqi turn me down.' In the end the rain drove me in
and I sat in my armchair testing the phone at intervals
to see if it was working. Picking it up, putting it down.
Random absurd compacts with fate – 'If when I look
at my watch it is past 5 o'clock, there's no hope.' And
yet in part of me hope was very strong. Another voice
inside me said loud and clear, 'This will work. They
will take it. It will come right.' But time slipped on,
past 5.15, past 5.30 … Too late, I thought. They have
gone home.

But sometimes hope is stronger than the dead fall
of failure, the weight in the heart, the bitter taste rising.
Because at 5.40 the phone rang again, and there was
Mai's singsong voice: 'We have had our meeting, and
I am ringing to say Yes, we would like very much to
publish your novel, if we can come to an agreement …'
We finished off with compliments – looking forward.

In fact, I was 'struck down, pole-axed. Floored by emotion, almost
exhaustion, almost blankness, something I could hardly give a name
to, but which possessed me, beyond words. I didn't know what to do
with myself.' (I see now it was like the aftermath of the endoscopy
which began this book: my body was left behind by my mind; it
had to find itself again.)

I felt I had to move, to go out, to walk, to find people,
to shout, to dance, to sing. I ended up walking down
the road under an extraordinary thunderstruck black-

and-sun sky, in the teeth of an icy wind, headed for my friend Hanna's, bits of whose life and wisdom are in that book – rang at her door, the doorbell was run down – they were out. Maybe in a way that was better, because I was in such a strange stunned state ...

Then I walked through hard cold rain to Willesden, foraging for my fair folk – I had a ten-pound note and some change in my pocket; bought a bottle of cheap fizz, a pizza for Rosa, mushrooms, good bread – thinking 'feast-time, feast-time, happiness'.

Walking back home from the bus down Liddell Gardens there was a blaze of late warm-toned sun and suddenly the Victorian school for the disabled was lit with red beauty – warm, warm, reaching up to the rain-cleared sky. I just stood and gazed; the sun, which had already set at my eye-level, shone above me in a high red band; it caught and lit the top of a tree of blossom; as I looked at the heights of the burning school, a small dark bird swooped up and over, made for the tower on the roof with a weather vane, and before my eyes landed on the very top in the sun – Hurrah, bird of my heart, well aimed.

And then down the long straight street of gardens towards my home, and everything was all at once illuminated with the joy I was too overcome to feel at first. The sky – such a sky. Pearly complicated clouds with a patch of warm sandy-gold and high fans of whitish silver, too bright to look at long, and behind them the pure thin blue – cherry trees that looked black against the sky until you got close and looked up and there as your blindness peeled away they were, deep maroon leaves and keen pink blossoms, nothing was black, everything swam with colour – and the sharp fresh smell of the altar of redcurrant flowers pulled me

across the wet road to bury my face in them – I wanted
to live for ever.

Yes: the joy. I can still feel it. It was not about money. It was the
work. The work, in which I'd put my soul and my heart, the bird
on its arc across the thin blue sky.

(But what if I had not had a friend? What if Moris Farhi had
not known Mai?)

Nearly a year later, I was in Australia with Rosa, a month or so
before *The White Family* was published. We were happy, on bikes,
a late balmy afternoon, tied them up and went into an internet café.
I opened Hotmail and saw a puzzling blizzard of emails. Most of
them were headed 'Congratulations ...' The book had been long-
listed, pre-publication, for the Orange Prize, the global prize for
women writing in English. It came out on that ready-made wave of
approval, and gained excellent reviews. Then, to the excitement of my
publisher and my triumphant, unreasonable joy, it was shortlisted.
And then, again, it was shortlisted for the International Dublin
Impac Award of 100,000 Euros, the largest award for a single book,
and ran into many editions and translations. I suppose you could
say I was vindicated.

The 'Disaster' years came more or less exactly in the middle of
my career to date, with my sixth, out of twelve, books (this is my
thirteenth). It turned out to be the middle, but it could have been
the end. Ever after, my memory of that time has added a resonance,
a shading, a depth of pleasure when good things happen; each time
a new foreign right is sold, each time I get the chance to travel for
my writing. Since the 'Disaster' years, I have been asked, for work,
to Rome, Munich, Stuttgart, Leipzig, Berlin, Paris, Vienna, Beirut,
Majorca, Ankara, Istanbul, Zurich, Tripoli, Geneva, Copenhagen
... so many foreign cities. So little time on this beautiful planet, and

writing is helping me travel around it. A new and quite unexpected African connection opened up for me in 2003 when my enterprising editor, Anna Wilson, said the right thing to Cheltenham Literary Festival, and they sent me to Kampala, Uganda, on an exchange with the Ugandan novelist Ayeta Anne Wangusa, which inspired friendships, short stories, two novels. My luck, my luck, sitting writing in Kampala with the weaver birds darting outside the open door. When, in 2004, I became Chair of the Council of the Royal Society of Literature, the first woman to hold that post, it meant more to me because, not so long before, I thought my life as a writer might be over.

Yet it is all a castle of air and spun sugar. I know now how frail it is, how quickly it shatters. My publisher is a small independent, one of the midget weightlifters still taking the strain of sustaining serious literature and scholarship here. Small, in their case, means strong and flexible, but flabby giants throw their weight about more, manipulate big sales, monopolise the book chains, pay for the best displays and pre-fixed places in the book-charts. I have not seized the handholds that make you safe 'for ever': winning a major prize, having a major bestseller (though as I write, Saqi have just sold the film-rights to my first African novel, *My Cleaner*.) My twelve books look solid enough, on the shelf, with their avatars, in thirteen languages, and there, among them, after long travail, *The White Family* and *The Ice People*, paid for in pain, repaying with a lesson ... But I take a deep breath, and touch the wood of my desk. There is still a great deal of work to be done.

And I shiver, and stare at the blank page of the future.

15 The stars leave the stage

en route for stardust

In the autumn of 1990, when Rosa was nearly four, there was a phone call to our London flat that sent me plunging down deep deep into a black pit of fear and grief and guilt. Dad came on first: 'Mum has something to tell you.'

Cancer. My mother's voice, a little hoarse, terribly truthful, spoke words in my ear that could not be taken back, that were changing life for ever, tick-tocking into my ear in the dark bedroom, while from our front room, sounds of impossible family happiness, suddenly now in the past, floated through – Nick had just come back from a trip to America, he and Rosa were tucked up on the sofa oblivious, watching *The Sound of Music. 'Climb every mountain, cross every stream, follow every pathway, till you find your dream.'*

My mother's favourite song from the film. But she had deferred all her dreams, all the things she wanted to do, all the places she wanted to go, until my father was dead, when she would be free. Now she was telling me the bitter truth. She had cancer. It would never happen.

Why was I guilty? Because (although this is pure superstition) I had been out of touch for two months, which was for ever, measured by the normal rhythm of communication with my parents. We wrote to each other every week, to reassure each other, we experts in the art of 'fit and well'. It was my father's habitual opener in phone calls, a plea or pre-emptive strike, not an open-ended question: 'So, Margaret, you're fit and well?'

But for some time I had not been fit and well at all; semi-paralysed, flattened like grass, by RSI. I was wired with pain, sapped of all strength. There was simply no vocabulary for conveying this news to my parents, even if I were able to write a letter, and to phone and say nothing seemed as bad as a lie. So I did not phone. Sudden radio silence.

Till my mother broke it with dread news. She too had stayed silent, while fear turned slowly into certainty. Then feeling for a way, herself, to break our rigid family conventions. To speak about the unspeakable, cancer.

My fault, I thought. All my life I'd half-believed my love had kept my mother alive. For eight weeks I had let her go. And now she phoned and told me she had cancer.

Quite soon my younger brother and I were on a train to Norfolk, coming to visit my mother in hospital after her operation. Afraid of the new unthinkable reality, that Mum might die. Clutching each other's arms as we walked down the long room towards her, beds of pained strangers to either side.

She did not die.

It was a very long convalescence. She stayed in hospital for months, and my sturdy, physically fit, bike-riding mother for a little while lost all confidence. I remember encouraging her to come out of the ward into the sunlight for a walk. I'd found a door that opened from the corridor onto the hospital garden and a bright fresh day, I wanted her to escape for a moment, and my mum, who had always longed to be up and away, clutched my arm like a different person, a different body – no, her own hurt body. 'I don't know, Margaret.' And came so slowly, her first trip outside after the terrible delvings and cuttings of the surgeon, feeling that her body might simply fall apart if removed from the sealed fug of safety.

A fortnight before she came home, Dad and I were summoned to see the consultant. The operation had been 'a success', but the cancer had spread to her liver. 'Two spots on her liver.' What did that mean? I asked. He gave us to understand that liver cancer was not considered to be treatable. But were they large spots? I asked. It sounded like such a small thing, two spots. You could take a rubber and rub them out. Then my father was asking how long she had got. The conversation seemed more and more unreal as the consultant, who I remember as thin and bald and blank, a mere cipher for death, was closing all the doors and windows on my mother's life – 'Between six months and a year.' I wanted my father to protest, but, probably in shock, he sat there silent. Then the consultant asked if we felt my mother should be told. I started to say that she should, but my father said she should be allowed to recover first, and then – 'You will tell her in your own time,' the consultant said.

Afterwards we sat outside in the sun. I said, 'Poor Mum, I can't believe it.' My father said, 'Well with the Parkinson's' – he had been diagnosed four years earlier, and his mobility had steadily declined, he had suffered mini-strokes and a mild heart attack –'I've probably not got much more than a year myself.'

'But she doesn't have to die just because you do!' I said, outraged. I was crying, he seemed impassive. Did he not love her enough to allow her her own existence, independent of his? Why didn't he grieve that her life, too, was ending? All I could think was that he was revealed in that moment as horribly selfish.

But of course she was his wife. What he spoke was just a reflex thought, a measuring out of their lives, side by side. He was probably asking himself the question that is posed by all long marriages: who will grieve for whom? Who will be alone? He said, 'We needn't tell her yet.'

In me there was just a voice howling *Mum, Mum*. Whose wit and intelligence and strength had always been fatally compromised by her fearfulness. Who could not stand up for herself and so had put off everything she hardly dared to hope for into the future, when Dad would be dead. And now her future was shrivelling, vanishing, gone, like the food in the fridge she had saved too long for it ever to be eaten. All an illusion.

My own delusion, which became an obsession, was that I must at least make sure Mum knew how little time she had left. I thought then she could decide how to spend it, was determined she should not be cheated, by Dad and the doctors, of this last chance.

So I tried to tell her. I tried every way I could to tell her the cancer was not cured, there were spots on her liver, her time was short. She refused to hear me. She became, for her, uncharacteristically angry. 'You could die before me, Margaret.' To say this to her own daughter whom she loved, her anger must have been beyond bounds. I was wrong, as so often in my life, completely and utterly. If she had known how bad things were, she could not have recovered. To live she needed hope. And I, who loved her, who believed I loved her more than anyone else, so nearly, and wrongly, took that hope away. I saw it as my duty to everything I knew about her, to her dreams, to her secret individual self, to her clear, undeluded intelligence; I thought I owed it to the pact between us, two women in this family of men. I was desperate to be truthful even though every cell in my body was electric with the pain I must give her. But it was like beating a stick against resistant silence; her will not to hear had the invisible strength of rubber. In the end I had the sense to respect it. Sometimes all that you know counts for nothing, because the world has changed behind your back.

Slowly, she fought her way back to fitness. Through a long summer. She was cooking again. (I judged my father harshly for that. Now I think we should judge no one harshly; the facts of life and death are harsh enough. I dare say she wanted normality back.) She was walking to the village again, then cycling, then driving.

At first, in my mind, the sands of time were running like blinding white rain. A dementing curtain of silica, constantly in motion, distracted me from everything beyond it, crazed the real picture of my mother (who was thinner than usual, quieter than usual but herself, steadying herself, still there, *still here*. Who was reading again, laughing at the political sketches in the *Guardian*, out in her red puffa jacket, walking only a little slower than before.) For a while I couldn't see her as she was, and enjoy her. That sibilant 'six months' had buried everything in dry, milling fear.

But for our own protection, fear is usually self-limiting. When for a brief period I suffered from panic attacks, it was comforting to read that the body is physically incapable of sustaining terror for more than about twenty minutes. You just have to put your head down and get through it.

The same held true on the bigger scale. After a few months of terror, I began to forget. Mum was putting on weight, looking better. Slowly and then faster, milestone followed milestone. Six months came and passed. Then a year. At some point she learned, not from me but a doctor, that there was some involvement of the liver, but I don't know exactly how frank they were, and I don't know how fully she accepted it. My mother was always an optimist; it was one of the lovable things about her, the many, many lovable things, for did she ever know how much I loved her? I think she did. I often told her.

Our visits relaxed into something like what they had been before, though Dad's increasing blindness meant we could not stay in the house, since blind people need everything to be in its place, and Rosa was an active five-year-old.

A restored near-normality. Miraculous.

The balance of power between my parents reverted. As my mother grew stronger, my father grew weaker. Dad was again the ill one, baby and boss, Mum was the organising functionary, the strong one. Slowly but surely, month by month, Dad's Parkinson's began to move towards its endgame. His blindness, too, got worse; he saw light and dark shapes, but not much else; he would draw Rosa close to him, and

gaze past her face. He still went for his morning walks, and refused
a white stick, but a neighbour took my mother to one side and told
her they were all afraid of running him over, aware he could no long
see cars coming (but Vic's hearing remained supernaturally acute,
perhaps fine-tuned by listening out for subversion in the kitchen).
He grew thinner and frailer, and needed more clothes, layering
waistcoats and woollens under his tweed jacket, his red zipped
tracksuit top now like a second skin as he tried to keep warm in his
last summer. And then there was another winter to get through, with
no hope, now, of escaping to Portugal, with daylight diminishing
too early, and the raw bitter wind that comes howling from Siberia
and harrows the low, flat East Anglian land. Every morning, though,
Dad got up in the dark and did his exercises, standing on one leg to
tie each shoe up, making the effort, the tremendous effort, until he
could no longer tie his shoes. Dressed himself up, layer after layer,
and fought his way out into the featureless cold, not long after the
sun cleared the red-brick bungalows and neutered yew-trees, bent
forward like a sprinter, though his step was now tiny, uncertain,
delicate, as if a slight breeze might have blown him off course. Mum
was cutting up his food and feeding him, now. She told me she had
said to him once, knowing that he was getting weaker, and she had
cancer, 'Together we can still do anything.'

She showed love for him. She lived it out. And what do I know
of the love between them, that existed when no one else was there,
that somehow endured the rage and the fear?

I hope that at last my mother was not frightened, or at least no
longer frightened of him. In a way, they both got their wish, at last,
though getting their wish involved their death. Vic was looked after
like a baby, with no rival sibling to push him away. Aileen had a mate
who did not frighten her, as her father had once frightened her in
drink, as the healthy Vic sometimes frightened her in temper.

I have not really said how bad things were, though in many other houses things were worse.

Once, in the car – it was an accident, although they were rowing – he pushed my mother hard against the door and 'broke her teeth', she said: perhaps it was one tooth. This was in the months before she left. The dentist repaired it, but she had had enough.

This incident is what sticks in my mind from all the scuffles and fights that were like something a child would do in a painful, unmanageable rage. I pity him for having to be violent: no one wants to be violent. When he threw a plateful of food across the table, how desperate must he have felt? How reduced to the rage of a thwarted infant. The fact remains, he was bigger than my mother, and when he was angry, out of control, so I cannot altogether pity him. I suffered from her fear; was afraid with her, and for her. Not so much for myself, once I reached adolescence, because I knew I would go away. I can't even remember how old I was when he stopped hitting me (but isn't there something odd about the way people say a child is 'too old to be hit'? Does it mean 'best only to hit children when they are too small to hit you back'?) I do remember him knocking off my glasses at the tea-table, when I was a sullen fourteen-year-old, and my brave elder brother standing up for me. We children did stand up for each other.

So much easier for me to love my father, first when I was no longer living at home; secondly when he was no longer (I must believe) hitting my mother; thirdly when he was blind and weak and definitely not hitting anyone at all any more; and finally now he is dead. I am loving the man he would have wanted to be, and might have had a chance to be. It was for us, to support his wife and children, that he gave up the chance to be a photographer and shouldered the crippling weight of the day job, the teaching job that made him a part-time tyrant, a head teacher of the corporal punishment era who obsessively told his family about each caning, bringing the shame of that back home. 'You're John's tyrant, Vic.'

But he didn't want to be. Probably he should have been an artist, with his thin skin and keen apprehension of beauty.

And in many respects I identify. I too am a Gee, and not always easy to live with. Gees are wonderful in theory, but oppressive and abrasive in practice. Oversensitive perfectionists who can keep working for ever, Gees have to learn the concept of 'good enough', 'getting by' and 'leave well alone'. I have to learn them. I am learning still. My father never learned to leave people alone. He wanted more from them; restlessly, urgently, he demanded more than he could be given.

(The body, of course, is the sane limiter of the mind. I learned not to overwork through my body refusing. Once I used to work through the night until I finished a piece; I fooled myself I was a pioneer pressing on through the hours when other people slept. Alone down that lit-up wire above the void. What arrogance! One night I fell off into nothingness and could not get back up again. I came up to bed at five, as many times before, with the light cracking the curtains like an ill-timed migraine, crawled into bed beside my husband, curled into him as usual, tried to sleep. Instead I began shivering, at first a little, then helplessly, violently, as if I were having a fit. I could not stop, and my heart began racing. Nick woke up and tried to warm me. After half an hour, he called an ambulance. Two stout ambulance-women, loud cheery Londoners, were soon in the room. After about a quarter of an hour with my heart racing over 225 beats a minute, they dressed me up, put me in the ambulance on a monitor, and belted off to Central Middlesex Hospital, Park Royal. Before we got to the hospital, my heart kicked into a normal rhythm. The conclusion in my medical notes was sound: 'Exhaustion'. I have never tried to work through the night again. One day I will die, but I want to live.)

Did my father once have a similar experience? He too would never give up until something was done. Even after retirement, he painted as if he were going to the block next day, carrying on through mealtimes, the Ribena arriving like a procession of jewels, keeping him going as the light faded. But something had made him value sleep excessively. To my mother's unspoken distress (since they always had to go to bed together, just as they did everything else together), he had to be in bed every day by 9.30. He got up after my mother, around 7.30 to 8 am, so I make it he got ten hours of sleep; enough for a baby. Which in some respects is what he would have liked to be, safe in the dark with his wife, his mother.

She did as he asked and looked after him at home when he finally couldn't get up any more. He had tried to outwit his own death (for the Parkinson's never affected his brain) or perhaps to outpace it, getting to the tape before the stage of indignity and helplessness. On my last 'normal' visit he sat, reduced, a cold, swaddled stick-man too clenched to smile. 'I'm no good any more, Margaret,' he said. I should have just received the message he gave, a simple message that mattered to him, a stark truth he was brave enough to state. But instead I replied with dishonest love, 'Don't say that. We're glad you're still here.' About three weeks before he died, he tried to kill himself with whisky (which he never drank) and aspirin. All that happened was that he did not wake up until midday the next day, with a hangover. I don't think he considered my mother (who would have been implicated) or the children. It was the ruthless side of him; rough courage. He took on death, and lost. Then he asked his GP to help him out, and was indignant when refused. But the doctor did give him advice: 'Stop eating.' Dad did stop eating. Death hurried closer.

I was staying with my elder brother in Lincolnshire when my mother phoned. 'Come,' she said. 'Dad can't get up. I can't manage on my own.' She, who always managed, needed us at last.

The doctor had put him on a morphine pump, a little black-and-clear vial attached to a vein, fixed by the side of the bed where he lay. Dad did not really want his children there, but he accepted my mother needed me. He was no longer making the rules. I tried to tell him that I loved him. In the overheated house, death ground into gear, getting ready for the last assault. Shrunken as Dad was, he still seemed so strong.

My mother became desperate to get out of the house. Only an hour before he died, she made me go for a walk in the next-door field, leaving my father alone with the elderly home help, who was naturally unwilling to be left in charge, and I was very anxious, and eager to get back, but Mum doggedly wanted to stay out in the air. There was no sunshine, just a wide grey sky. We seemed dwarfed by it, in the empty field. Coarse grass, rugged cloud, red clover, and a death going on in the red brick box nearby. 'Mum, we *have* to go back.' Holding hands, we went back.

Till the end he kept surfacing, uneasy, desperate, and we were torn between pity and fear, and used the manual override on the pump to take him back down to oblivion. In the end, his strong body was overcome. His colour changed, suddenly yellow-white all over, and his hand, very quickly, felt icy cold.

His death was not calm, or kind, or resigned, but he died at home, as was his wish, protected from strangers, free of nurses. It was the end his own father had begged for: 'Don't let me go to Rennie Lodge, Aileen.'

At his funeral, all his children spoke. I chose Shakespeare's 'Fear no more the heat o' the sun.' He was a fearful man who no longer had anything to be afraid of; he was a brave man despite his fear; he had always, unstintingly, uncomplainingly, supported us. Home was what he lived for and he loved us absolutely, with a blind, worry-filled, concentrated love. He was fiercely proud of each one of us, and prayed for us each night on his knees, though he was too obstinate to go to church. His belief in me helped me to write. He told Aunty Kit I would be a great writer. My mother ferried this back to me, and though he was formally unqualified to make the judgement, that generous faith surged like a wave behind me.

I imagine my father slipping once again through the golden fields of grain between Stony Stratford and Wolverton, sloping home through the late sun, light on his small feet, stopping to dribble and kick a stone, his check Viyella shirt soft and warm on his neck, his pale blue painter's and meteorologist's eyes as keen as they were when he was a boy, enjoying and naming the gentle feathers of cirrus cloud high in the sky, nothing to worry about, no one to fret, the money he had earned a friendly weight in his pocket, going home for a rest now, Vic Gee of Wolverton, sure he would be welcome at last, going home.

> *Fear no more the heat o' the sun*
> *Nor the winter's barren rages.*
> *Thou thy earthly task hast done,*
> *Home art gone, and ta'en thy wages.*

Mum died exhausted, herself, six months later. At least she had lived alone, and for herself, for a while, and danced in the kitchen to her tapes, and come to London, and watched *The Sound of Music* tucked up in bed with her adored Rosa, and met my friends, who liked her; and at home, made a friendship, unmonitored by Dad, with her witty neighbour Janet, and rode her red bike, and drove off to Weybourne every morning before breakfast to go swimming.

And then there were the weeks we spent together, Mum and I, a final gift from the gods before everything was taken away. We had never had enough time *à deux*: never had a mum-and-daughter day out, or lunch out, let alone a mum-and-daughter holiday. Dad was jealous even of the coffees we had, at the Copper Kettle, in Billingshurst, when we were shopping. He would tap his watch: 'What took you so long?'

Now I came to stay with Mum on her own, and we had a month of amity and happiness, Marg and Mum, Mum and Marg. My husband let me go, as he always let me go, as Vic could never let Aileen go. I wrote in the day, in the warm cedar shed, and in the evening we

Mum explaining the world to me. She said, 'I grew up in the woods and fields. Scatter me in the woods and fields.'

ate delicious meals and drank sherry and watched TV. And my mother bought clothes. After a lifetime of 'not spoiling herself', she spent the small reserve of money in the bank on jackets and skirts and blouses, all in the bright colours she loved, mostly scarlet. Maybe she had a premonition, one of her rare and unlucky premonitions, that there would be no use for the money later.

On the station platform at Sheringham, seeing me off on an autumnal evening after the happy month we had spent together, a wintry chill in the air but the sky midnight blue and drenched with small bright stars, Mum held my hand in the dark. Our living hands, flesh over the bone. There weren't many passengers. The train was late. She said, 'I feel fine, let's wish for a couple of years. Three. Five.' 'Yes,' I said fervently. 'I'm wishing.' 'How about seven?' she said. 'Seven,' I agreed, clutching at her living hand, but the night felt cold, and inside me some voice was saying, 'Not seven', and the train for Norwich shunted into the station.

Three weeks after I went back to London, by a random side-blow of fate, perhaps through overworking on the novel in our first house, where the new central heating wasn't yet installed, I was in hospital with pneumonia, taken in as an emergency with a sky-high temperature and put on intravenous antibiotics while I lay there seeing visions of crystalline architecture that are, it seems, a side-effect of brain chemistry in fever. Coming out weak and thin, I had been home only a few days when I got the phone call from my mother. She had always asked for so little, but now she was urgent and direct, as only once before, when my father was dying. 'Margaret, please come. Will you come?'

Mum had woken up to find she had turned yellow, and was very afraid. She had arranged an appointment with the doctor, knowing that if this was jaundice, it probably came from her liver. After that call I went to Norfolk, and did not leave her.

Next day Mum's face was more yellow than before. We visited the surgery together. The doctor, who knew her history, looked stricken, but agreed there was more than one possible explanation. We begged for some that weren't cancer, and he gave them, but in his eyes we could see he did not believe them. 'Have you been losing weight?' he asked my mother. 'No,' she said. And then, 'Only a few pounds.' He was nodding his head. That was what he expected.

We went into the Norwich hospital, and they ran tests. We had prayed it was a random infection: there was no infection. As the results came in, the news grew steadily worse. We kept hoping, but every day there was less to hope for. Concentrated, hope became fiercer and more desperate, but began to be tinged with leaden despair. Mum had hoped for seven years; soon we hoped for months. And then for weeks, and then only days. At last there was nothing left to hope for, not even our desperate plan to get her out to spend a last Christmas with us in London. A last-ditch operation was too painful to endure; I suppose she was too ill for them to use general anaesthetic. They had to stop, in mid-session, trying to introduce a stent which would have helped her liver manage for a few more weeks. She was brought back to the ward, dark with pain.

In her remaining days, she wrote kind, bright letters, in her normal firm and impeccable hand, some to people who'd been too afraid to come to see her once they knew that she was dying. The family arrived, and sat around the bed, and my mother managed to laugh with them. My brothers came, and Mum's beloved grandchildren. Mum's ability to enjoy herself, anywhere, at any time, bubbled up, miraculous. She let my daughter feed her grapes. As she floated away, in the end, on morphine, time circled back to its beginning, to that graveyard opposite the tiny house in London Road, Stony Stratford, where she grew up with all those brothers and sisters, and she saw the 'women in long white dresses' she remembered from the years after the First World War, and her own mother, May, gentle mouth and dreamy eyes, the person of whom she remembered only kindness; and she said the phrase I can never forget, 'There's someone waiting for me at home who's good as gold, good as gold.' I sat by her bedside, by then on my own, on that long last night, stroking her hand. For her it was a comfort, going home, but in retrospect it made me afraid, since I never, for myself, want to go back home, if home means the family I grew up in.

'You're my rock,' she said, not long before she died. But she had to say goodbye to me.

Neither of us thought this was possible. We had loved each other dearly, deeply, always. When she was in her seventies, and I in my forties, we would walk along the village road hand in hand. She had put up with all my adolescent hatred, my tangled love life, my absurdities. She knew me through and through, and loved me, though she half-pitied Nick, I think, for marrying me, because she knew I could be difficult. Yet we were the women in the family. We were the deepest and most intimate friends. We looked into each other's eyes and saw everything, always. How could death part us? 'I'll wait for you,' she said to me. 'You'll come, won't you, before too long.' 'Not yet ...' I drew back a little, afraid.

And then she said the thing that still haunts me with mingled grief and happiness. 'If I get there, I'll let you know. If I get there, I'll wait for you.'

Is she waiting, somewhere? Where do they go?

How long will it be before the call comes?

The stars leave the stage, one by one. The aunts, the uncles, the fixed points of childhood.

Mum was right, of course. There's not long to wait between the deaths of child and parent, not long *sub specie aeternitatis*. Logically, the length of a generation. You can work it out, a macabre kind of maths. If I die at the age my mother was, I have to add on her age when I was born – thirty-three – to the date of her death. Which would see me joining her, or setting off to find her, in 2025, fifteen years hence. It doesn't seem very far away. I hope for more, am afraid of less.

I missed my mother, and grieved for her, for all the things she had dreamed of doing. I do them partly for her, now. I think how pleased she'd be to see me travelling, and fly with her flight bag, unglamorous but practical, an indestructible black-and-red 'Samsonite' shoulder bag that makes me feel she's coming with me. She's come with me to Africa, Australasia.

1992 was the year I grew up, if grief is what makes you grow up. Both my parents died in the same year. I was forty-three for one, forty-four for the other: old enough to bear it, at least. Children have to lose their parents, it's natural, though it feels like a violation, at the time. The other way round is even harder. I had a miscarriage that year, as well.

Where do they go? Unborn children. They are wanted and expected, but never come.

And those who have lived solidly here on earth, who were part of our lives, who should always be there – Peg, Gwynneth, Aileen. Vic and Tennant. Aunty Eve and Aunty Bertha. Lloyd and Hilda and the grandparents. My brilliant young commissioning editor from the 1990s, Jonathan Warner, who tried too hard to make everything perfect. Dear Christine Casley, with her dreamily amused, husky voice and blue eyes and elegant, youthful bob, my editor for *The Ice People* and *The White Family* and *The Flood*, who I stupidly expected to be there for ever, like a sharpened reflection of my consciousness as, deeply attuned, she shaped and sifted; with her youthful gift of pleasure in everything – flowers, pictures, the lunches we shared; but she died in months of a brain tumour. And Beverly Hayne, my almost-cousin, so funny and stroppy and sharp and bright, and fine-grained, melancholy Kitty Mrosovsky, who died because she had the wrong boyfriend, and Nina, after a long struggle with lupus started by a random shard of glass on a beach. Four beautiful, distinctive voices I can hear still, plaiting together as they stretch away from me into nothingness, almost gone, and I strain after them, missing them. The living who die, and the never-arrived. The mystery is, where do they go?

Where have they gone, who were so alive? *Ubi sunt.* The lament of generations, the poets grieving for us all.

What is a soul? When my mother died, around 5.30 in the morning, just before the first light leaked into the ward, there was an absolute sense that someone had *gone.* Wherever she was heading, she had quietly set off, leaving nothing on the bed but a pile of clothes. Her breathing had gradually grown quieter. It was a far gentler death than my father's. I kissed her cold face, I kissed her hand, but of her it was the merest simulacrum. As the long night ended, she slipped from the stage, and I began the decades of my life without parents.

16 My animal luck (viii)

We are each other –
'we are each other's parents'[*]

It was because of Nick that I did not feel an orphan, though I missed my mother painfully. He was there in the tiny cubicle room that the hospital provided for relatives, and as I slipped into the single bed we were sharing, at 6 am, as morning began, there was the wonder of his warm, tender body, and I cried against him, my tears on his skin, and we made love, and I fell asleep exhausted, but when I woke up, the worst horror had gone. When my mother-in-law died, his lovely, lively, unconventional mother Peg, we were still relatively recently married, and her death made me realise how much I loved him as he trusted me with his grief, and we shared it.

In a way I had always missed my mother, ever since childhood when I took her for granted. So many times in my adult life she could not be there, because of Dad's rules, because they always had to come as a pair, and as a pair, they made me anxious. When I gave birth, when I got married, I loved my mother, I missed my mother.

I shan't write very much about my marriage, because it is dangerous to write about the living. I have asked my daughter, and got her permission for 'anything between birth and adolescence': I tell my

---

* From a poem by Christopher Reid.

two brothers I will love them and leave them out, because their stories are theirs, not mine. My husband has given me *carte blanche*, but how can you write about a twenty-six-year marriage? It is a space where we are safe to love. I love having it, and fear losing it, or Nick losing me, leaving him alone.

I say that as an offering to the universe, conceding that happiness is always perilous, and I am grateful for what we have. Yes, quarrels, explosions, days of stormy temper, days when I can't imagine why I married this man, and he can't imagine why he married me. And yet, such animal happiness, such fun and permission, such infinite freedom. The joys of insults, and friendly abuse. The times when we are like jostling siblings, and the times when lots of incest is nicest. Long sunlit mornings in the marital bed. The constant pleasure of talking, listening, sifting the beaches of each day's meaning. That he is me, and I am him.

When I was little, I used to wish my bed was a boat, rounded off to a prow that would float through the night, bob over the waves, rock me awake in the morning. My boat was male, my boat was female, it blended adventure and the arms of my mother, holding me tenderly whatever happens. Though Nick is a very masculine man, in some ways he is both my father and mother, a better father than my father was, as good a mother as my mother was.

I cradle him. He cradles me. Our marriage is a boat where we bob together. We have passed many rocks, many bleak landscapes.

Reader, I meant to leave it at that. But my mother's dying left a long shadow. I had been too close; death breathed too hard. As I write about it, I long for life.

Reader, come with me, out of the dark. The blazing heat of full summer.

August 6, 1983. The sun shone down; we were touched by the gods. I took a train from London and met Nick in Cambridge. We had both dressed like cultists, without prior discussion, me in a long white satin antique nightdress, the only white thing I possessed, Nick in a loose white Indian overshirt and cheesecloth trousers, gathered at the ankles: to the casual observer, we were both in our pyjamas, but I was gilded at hand and foot, with a small gold bag, gold bangles, gold sandals. Like everything else, we did it by instinct. We had two witnesses, John Waite and Barbara Goodwin: he a youthful best man, she a mauve-and-silver bridesmaid.

The props were all in place for us. We needed flowers, had forgotten them, but a stall appeared by the side of the road we were tearing along to the registry office; our best man stopped his yellow car and I saw the gold chrysanthemums, great heavy-headed things on proud straight stems. I bought half a dozen, they were meant for me. They matched my hair, my gold haloes of bangles.

Our animal selves were jostling with the angels. My chaste white nightdress clung to my breasts. My yellow hair reached down my back, and Nick's was thick and deep brownish-black, long for a man, and he was bearded. He is very handsome, the camera shows, but what surges up still from the photographs is our hunger, our yearning; the love is palpable, a summer heat that shimmers off the skin of the image. We are drugged, drowning, drenched in each other. In one photo he is kissing me and I am pressed back, we are arched together, a bow of longing pointing to the future.

Our wedding day

We were tender, frightened, serious as we stood side by side and made our vows. Utterly possessed by the day and each other, although the meaning of what we had done was still mysterious to us. Oh animal life! Oh human ritual, striving to point our passions upwards. But it had a point, for we were also two souls, asking for a sign from the universe.

Barbara made the perfect photo as we half-ran, laughing, from the registry office. She asked John to throw a shower of confetti; it floated like blossom past the ugly brick, it stays there for ever in the eye of the camera, a canopy of stars over our frail bodies.

From the square modern building we fled back to nature. Our 'reception' (for four) was at a wooden picnic table in the summer-green Botanical Gardens. There must have been other people passing by, but they were pale silhouettes, invisible, silent. In the photographs, we four are alone. Nick and I have left the table and wander through the trees, or stand gazing at each other, amazed, a tiny couple in a lost savannah of sunlit grass and big sheltering trees. We are deaf and dumb; we are the first humans; life stretches all round us and will go on for ever.

17 What is a soul?

each living instance

Rosa was only five when they died, Grandpa and Grandma, in the same year. 1992 cast a little shadow across her life that is perhaps still there today; the ghost of a shadow, the knowledge of death. In the 'Autobiography' her secondary school encouraged her to write, aged thirteen, she wrote a chapter called 'The Year of Tragedies'.

Of course you have to say goodbye to the past. But that year, we also said goodbye to the future.

The year began with a lost child. No funeral, no body, just a burying of dreams. I miscarried on my father's birthday, February 14, a Saturday, at nine or ten weeks. Not my last miscarriage, my second. I was almost used to it, knew it from before, a gathering dread that things weren't going right – the sickness lessening (for sickness is a good sign), the dull return of normality, my breasts no longer throbbing: the failure to transform. Another D and C. Forcing the anaesthetist to acknowledge my grief, for he had been laughing with me (in kindness) on the way to the ward, as the needle slipped into a vein on my wrist I said to him clearly and urgently, feeling it must be recorded or whoever had been precariously alive would twice die, 'I want you to know that I wanted this baby.'

The first time it happened is the clearest in my mind. Long hoped for, already much loved; the silver and black ghostliness of the scan we thought would be routine, but which showed no life, nothing, no heartbeat, no more hope. 1989. Poor Nick, who was late after parking the car, or else they sent me in early, knocking harder and harder on the door of the ultrasound room at the hospital to get in; that was worse than the pain for myself, having to tell him, strangled with tears, 'I'm so sorry,' I said, 'so sorry.' Knowing how blindly and deeply it would hurt him.

It hurt Rosa too. She was only three; people said, 'too young to understand', but they were wrong. She both understood, and misunderstood in ways that might have poisoned our whole relationship insidiously had she not had the genius to enact what was in her mind.

At first she felt, or showed, only sorrow, and pity for me. I still have the thing she made to console me. Unbelievably, she drew a baby on kitchen paper, about the size a newborn baby would be, but with short arms that made the whole thing like a cross with a heavy head, came through and laid it in my arms as I lay in bed in our bedroom with its windows opening over the grass, the greenness, the pointless blank and the blue: 'Here's a baby for you, Mummy.' And then as the days went on she became strange and evasive and did not want to be near me. When Nick went out she ran after him, clinging and crying. It was almost as if she was afraid of me, but that could not be so. Could it?

Then she showed me what was tormenting her by taking her toys, one after another, and hanging them from her upper bunk with scarves. I took them down and asked her why she was doing it. 'I just wanted to see what it was like,' she said, but she still wouldn't look me in the eye. 'What was it like?'

She thought I was killing the babies who died. Oddly, art helped, or symbolism did, at this bleakest of junctures, where nothing, you would think, could help. By a kindness of fate, or the pity of God, for surely only God could have such perfect pity – or because my longing was so deep and raw that it called forth what was needed from the universe, in which case the universe itself is God, which is what I mostly, most deeply, believe – the book opened, that evening, at bedtime, at a story we had never read, 'What Happened to the Unicorn?' by Jenny Koralek. I read it to Rosa, not knowing where it would take us, in much the same way as the child in the story, who has lost something and needs solace, wanders into a green wood. I cannot remember the details now, but I do remember there was a unicorn among the trees – that the child talked to it, and loved it – but the unicorn, magical as it was, was only here on a visit, could not stay. I think Rosa and I both knew, without words for the thing we knew, that the unicorn was a soul. The soul we longed for which had slipped away. The soul, the well-spring of loss and sorrow. And we were both crying as the story ended, tears which mended things; because Rosa was learning afresh that I mourned what might have been. I think from then on she was no longer afraid.

For us, someone living had died, though in each case the babies were less than three months. I support women's right to abortion as a very poor second to contraception, but I cannot accept that no one is killed. I don't buy the claim that the child in the womb is any less alive than the child outside. It would simply be more convenient for us if we didn't have to think of what we kill as living.

I have friends, atheist scientist friends, who stop still and physically stiffen if I inadvertently, in their presence, say something about the soul or the spirit. There's a war on, at present, between science and religion, only partly because of the advance of creationists. My generation took it for granted that the theory of evolution was true: who could really believe that, as the Bible says, the earth was made in only six days?

Yet can't scientists make a distinction between private and public kinds of knowledge? Do they feel, when someone near to them dies, that only something material is lost? Is one beloved dog the same as another?

I don't find it easy to define a soul, which is why I have left it till nearly last. In a way my own formal beliefs are not useful, because they exist in a different space. I was confirmed into the Church of England. What do I cling on to, of those beliefs? I think Jesus Christ is a perfect model: of kindness, empathy, lack of pride. His parables speak to the artist in me, as do the beauty of the hymns and the psalms. My father's love for 'Morning has broken/Like the first morning,' is everyone's love of, and longing for, renewal; his desire for a new self is my own. I am moved by Matthew Fox's version of the faith, where the *anawim*, the humble and excluded, are always at the core of it. *The first shall be last. Be as little children.* A mirror reversal of the world we know, quietly radical, the gentlest miracle. An image, an otherworld that hangs there, beckoning, beyond the hills of hurt and worry. I take communion, though rarely; I kneel with others to say we are linked, this is the face of the faith I grew up in. I sit, grateful to be welcomed.

But since I was sixteen, and 'lost my faith', I cannot literally believe in a paradise with God and Jesus and the saints: *where would it be?* is my problem. Where am I to imagine them? It falls apart, it turns to cardboard. More seriously, for this means that most Christians might see me as inimical, I cannot believe that there is only one God who happens to focus on our planet, our species, one species among so many species, one tiny planet in this vast universe of galaxies and stars and countless planets which surely, certainly harbour other life-forms. Why would that wide glory of light, space, matter, have a God centred on our little earth? Our Christian God looks suspiciously like us. If God exists, he must have many faces, so everyone can find their own face. Besides, as I learn about other faiths, I see they have aspects of the same beauty, speak to the same needs and longings. It isn't only Christians who value compassion, love, forgiveness, charity. Who speak to the best in us, and face the worst.

I think of the Thai pendant I wore on the night when I felt I was saved by an answer to prayer, when the conscript threatened to rape and kill me. At the time, I had no idea what it meant, whose image it was. I bought it as fashion. Only writing this book have I realised that I wore on my breast that fateful night the Buddhist Goddess of Compassion, Kuan Yin, who is described as 'an incarnation of Mary', whose person embodies loving kindness. Kuan Yin hears the cries of the suffering; her name means 'she who hears the sounds of the world'. She is said to have refused to enter heaven when the cries of the living came to her ears. Which compassion saved me? Kuan Yin's, or Jesus's? I would say, compassion in the universe; though in another universe, perhaps I was killed, in the universe I live in now, I was saved. But behind that larger claim there are real, small facts: compassion from the French boys who worried about me, who came and interrupted what was happening; my own compassion for myself, which made me hold on and hold off my attacker; even some buried restraint or pity in him which stopped him raping me straightaway. (But think also of those who are not saved, who are cruelly killed, tortured, murdered, who suffer for years, with no remission, who pray in terror and are not answered.)

I would say that life split in two that night, is always splitting, an infinite regression, and that often I have been in the luckier half, often my need has called forth an answer – when the young Frenchmen arrived to save me, when my rejected novels were finally accepted. Because of the images I grew up knowing, the face of compassion for me is Jesus, but who is the god of birds and insects, or of the life-forms who were once on Mars? I believe that God is in all of them. I feel God is in each living instance. And so I return to my quest for the soul.

Perhaps it is the organism's track through time and space, its particular, detailed, unrepeatable plait of image, memory, and emotion? Its unique path through the universe, even if that is only across a village, across a field, across a stone: or briefly flickering inside another's body, carried wherever the mother goes. Maybe all memories are inscribed somewhere – some say they are coded in the proteins of the brain, that everything is there but ninety-nine per cent of it is stored invisibly and silently, or we would be maddened with memory, like Borges's character, Funes the Memorious. When

Catching the light

the organism dies, all its memories are lost, and that is part of the ache of bereavement.

My name for what slips out of reach is a soul. Its lustre comes from our love of it, our helpless sorrow when it has gone.

Respect for other living things – the respect that should always be there, but which fails us – might be easier to maintain if we granted every other being a soul: what my hero Kurt Vonnegut's invented artist, Rabo Karabekian, described in *Breakfast of Champions* as 'an unwavering band of light', invisible but real, shining at the centre of us all.

For me it is also the net of connections that haloes every consciousness, linked to the future as well as the past, streaming both towards and outwards from our bodies. It's our sensitivity to what's outside us: pain and joy, beauty and horror, a capacity that differs for every living thing. It's also our power to generate surprise: to move at a tangent, to be ourselves, to sing, bark, swing, laugh, play, sulk, fall, to improvise our role in the great living tapestry that makes our planet extraordinary, its whole restless surface a sea of souls. Babies in the womb are already unpredictable, kicking and turning, dancing on their cord, and then sometimes that sensation, magical but brief, that Fay Weldon wrote about in her novel *Puffball*: sometimes, inside me, the baby was happy; as Weldon describes it, the baby is laughing; the glory of laughter not laughed by me. And every animal on the planet emanates livingness, which is change. In that uniqueness, the soul pulses.

And that is why killing is the great taboo. For humans, at least, of other humans. But we deem non-human animals less living than ourselves, so we can farm them and kill them for our use.

When my mother died, I felt lonely because she could no longer react to me, or enjoy change, or look forward to things. Because my mother would never be there again. I would remember her, and I would love her, and I would try to tell her story. But her soul was not with me, and so I was lonely. And so was everyone who loved my mother.

When the embryos inside me died, we sorrowed because they had lost their future, they had slipped silently into dead matter, their bright capacity for change was stilled. We had lost the mystery of their transformation, and with that, we lost part of ourselves, the part that had hoped to move into their future, and our darling daughter went on alone. Infinitely precious: alive, alive, with her generous capacity to surprise, as she placed the frail cut-out child in my arms, and her love wished a soul into that crumpled paper.

Ubi sunt? Where do they go?

If I knew, I would tell you. I would go to find them. I would meet my mother, as she said we would. And yet I am not ready to go beyond, to that place from which it seems we cannot come back. Do they look across the bourn? Do they still see us?

All I know is that my parents, my grandparents, my aunts, my little band of dear dead friends exist somewhere, as long as I do, transformed into longing and regret, which brightens, at times, into happiness. For they were here, when I was here. We saw each other, we held each other.

I think of Turner's Italian paintings, which I have just seen again in Edinburgh, drawn by his skill with tiny, far-off detail – he sometimes used a very fine reed pen. The effect of this is astonishing.

Distant islands of sharpness emerge from his mists, clearer and more compelling than his foregrounds. That restored completeness speaks to my desire. As if parts of the past hold more light than the present – an energy which could bear them on into the future. It is not a mirage, it floats there intact, a blue sunlit shore beyond the grey middle ground where a tiny band of souls is still waiting to go forward, about to set sail across the evening for Venice. An afterlife that Turner has saved from dissolution. It shines in water, like a lost pearl necklace.

There is a bleaker strait where it is hard for me to go. It is a place of unknowing, where only pain is. Though I see how in the scheme of things – whatever that phrase means – *it's an apology, a lie* – though in the lying scheme of things, our grief was as nothing, or something small – though other people's pains are often much greater, I yield to them, concede to them – though I agreed blindly when kind friends said, 'You are very lucky, you have one daughter', though the logical side of me assents to this – part of me has never 'got over' the miscarriages; 'got over', as if they were a stone in the road; as if my mind had returned them to the non-living. I did not know them; I could not touch them. But they lived in me, and were real to me, and in this blind mad part of me, which I never let out into the light, I believe that as I die I will find those children. They will wait for me, and I will hold them. I will know them. I will love them. They will not be lost, for how can they be lost, for if souls can be lost …?

I don't know the ending.

18 My animal luck (ix)

the dance, the dance

I don't know the ending. Because there is none, until our planet is absorbed by our star. Our lives are so short, a breath, half a breath. This moment soaking up the sun.

Here and now. The bright shock of the present. I began this memoir two years ago, at St Cuthman's retreat, near Billingshurst and the ghosts of my girlhood, the village where I lived from seven to seventeen, and I end it in a second retreat, in Hawthornden, Scotland, which is free of memories and ghosts. Perhaps I am freeer than when I started. I look back on the life I have written down, brief bits of a path mostly hidden by trees. I was given much; I have little to forgive.

Another bee is fumbling outside the window, a big heavy visitor, trying to get in. All round me, glorious April has begun. Spring is running away towards summer. The buds of the sycamores along the winding drive were like pale yellow pointed light-bulbs when I got here, slanted every which way on the black wire twigs like the snake of lights on our Christmas tree. But already they have burst into pleated green fans, miniature fingers pushing eagerly outwards, and the bud-cases lie like small wings on the ground. I must not think, as I see the sap rising, that if I die at the same age as my mother, there will only be fifteen more springs. Stay in this moment, the budding moment, the day still pregnant with tomorrow.

My animal luck: my living body. The living bodies of my husband, my daughter. The chain of three hundred generations of couples, linked in the dance, in the heat of the bed, all of whom were lucky, who begat children. Link after golden link: my luck.

Thank you, my parents, my grandparents. The two families who joined in me, and before them four, eight, sixteen …

All that fucking. That blood, that heat. That animal life. Quarrels, laughter, but the business of pushing life on got done.

Thank you, my friends, my dearest friends. Barbara and Hilary, my sisters, Jim and Grania and all the others who proved to me what kindness was. Thank you my teachers, who saw something in me, that white-haired, skinny, solemn child with her sudden fits of dancing and laughter. Thank you, Mai, who is just out of reach, and Musa, and André, for saving my writing.

Thank you, Rosa, for being my heart. It is too full to say any more. Thank you, Nick, for giving me Rosa. Thank you, Nick, for my animal bliss, for sharing this life with me, this breath.

Before I go, before you go, I place my story in your hands, the wonder of your living hands.

This have I done for my true love.

Tomorrow shall be my dancing day.
I would my true love did so chance
To see the legend of my play,
To call my true love to the dance.

Sing, oh! my love, oh! my love, my love, my love,
This have I done for my true love.

(Anon)

Acknowledgements

Grateful thanks to Nick McDowell and Arts Council England for their belief and support. *My Animal Life* was finished at Hawthornden International Writers' Retreat: I would like to thank Dame Drue Heinz, Dr Martin Gaskell and the staff for their kind hospitality.